Succeed with

FRENCH GRAMMAR

by
Talia Bachir

in collaboration with
Isabel Langenbach

BARRON'S

First edition for the United States and Canada
© Copyright 2007 by Barron's Educational Series, Inc.
Original edition © Copyright 2005 by Ernst Klett Sprachen GmbH,
Stuttgart, Federal Republic of Germany. All rights reserved.

Author: **Talia Bachir**
Collaborator: **Isabel Langenbach**
English translation: **Eric Bye**

All inquiries should be addressed to:
Barron's Educational Series, Inc.
250 Wireless Boulevard
Hauppauge, NY 11788
http://www.barronseduc.com

ISBN-13: 978-0-7641-3658-0 (book only)
ISBN-10: 0-7641-3658-5 (book only)
ISBN-13: 978-0-7641-9340-8 (book & CD package)
ISBN-10: 0-7641-9340-6 (book & CD package)
Library of Congress Control Number: 2006929365

Printed in Canada
9 8 7 6 5 4 3 2 1

Welcome to the world of French grammar!

Would you like to learn French grammar quickly, with enjoyment, and enthusiasm? Would you like to understand the rules thoroughly and be able to apply them?

In this course you will learn the most important grammatical features of the language. You will work intensively with the grammar using a modern, communication-based method, and will learn how to apply it in lifelike situations. At the same time you will acquire a solid basic knowledge of communication, vocabulary, and geography through a variety of exercises. Because of its flexible approach, *Succeeding with French Grammar* is appropriate for both beginners and for people who have had some prior exposure to the language. Answer keys and tips help you to master French grammar more quickly as an independent learner.

How is *Succeeding with French Grammar* structured?

Succeeding with French Grammar consists of 12 modules and 12 tests. Each module begins with an easy introduction to the various subjects. There are also clear explanations, and you have the opportunity to use what you have learned in numerous exercises. After every module you can take a test to see if you really have mastered the contents.

The course is complemented by an audio CD; it contains lots of the exercises and provides thorough practice for your listening comprehension, pronunciation, and oral communication.

The exercises are numbered sequentially so it's easier for you to find where you are at a glance. This will also help you in checking the answers that are located in the appendix of the book.

Graphic Symbols

Using the graphic symbols you can tell if you need a pencil, an extra piece of paper, or the audio CD (always optional) for any given exercise:

 This symbol shows you that the exercise is also on the audio CD. The track number tells you where to find the exercise on the CD.

 For an exercise with this symbol you need a pencil to write something down or to fill in something.

 You also need a pencil for these exercises, this time to check something off or to connect items.

With this symbol you are invited to use an additional piece of paper in doing the exercise.

 This symbol notifies you that you should pay particularly close attention to the material.

Bon à savoir !

The following nouns exist only in the plural:
les lunettes –
the glasses
les toilettes –
the toilet

The box contains useful, interesting notes about the French language and country-specific details.

Translations of popular sayings:
1. *I think, therefore I am.*
2. *When the cat's away, the mice will play.*

The vocabulary field contains words and expressions that are helpful in the relevant exercises.

aller	
je vais	nous allons
tu vas	vous allez
il va	ils vont

This box contains verbs in their conjugated forms.

Appendix

Here you will find the following:

Answers:	You can refer to the appendix to check your answers.
Grammar:	Here you will find thorough explanations of all the important grammar covered in this course.
Glossary:	In the alphabetical glossary you can quickly find all the words used in *Succeeding with French Grammar* along with their translations.

Have fun, and lots of luck learning French!

Table of Contents

Contents

1

Here you see Mounir, who is waiting for Marie in the Café Rose.
Which words in the picture are feminine, and which are masculine?
Put them into the chart.

masculine	feminine

un serveur – une serveuse – un étudiant – une étudiante – une bière –
Mounir – un pastis – un journal – une table – une chaise

2 TR. 01

This involves the singular and the plural of the terms. Connect the
plural forms on the right with the appropriate singular forms on the left.
Pay attention to the ending of the plural form. You can also listen to the
words on the CD.

1. un serveur	a. des serveuses
2. un étudiant	b. des bières
3. une bière	c. des journaux
4. une table	d. des étudiants
5. une étudiante	e. des tables
6. une serveuse	f. des étudiantes
7. un journal	g. des pastis
8. un pastis	h. des serveurs

3 ✎

Masculine or Feminine?

In French all nouns are either masculine or feminine, usually without regard to their meaning. So for example, **la personne** (*the person*) can refer to a man. Fortunately, there are some rules to help identify the gender of these words.

The most common endings of masculine nouns are **-eur**, **-eau**, **-in**, **-ail**, and **-ment** and the most common feminine endings are **-e**, **-euse**, **-té**, **-ade**, **-tion**, and **-ette**.

The definite or indefinite article (**un**/**une**/**le**/**la**/**l'**) is usually placed before the noun. It is written with lowercase letters unless it is part of a proper name or a nationality.

Write the words on the appropriate lines:

Masculine: _____

Feminine: _____

> vendeuse – fromage – gâteau – matin – table – chaise –
> carte – travail – Française – serveur

4 TR. 02 👓

Nouns that designate people (or animals) often have a masculine and a feminine form. The feminine form can usually be derived from the masculine form. Look at the pairs of words. How can you tell that the second word is feminine? Read the applicable rules and pronounce the words, which you can listen to on the CD.

un Anglais ▶ une Anglaise	un Allemand ▶ une Allemande
un chien ▶ une chienne	un Parisien ▶ une Parisienne
un invité ▶ une invitée	un ami ▶ une amie
un célibataire ▶ une célibataire	un journaliste ▶ une journaliste

Generally the feminine form is made by adding the ending **-e**.

Special considerations:

masculine **-en**	▶ feminine **-enne**
masculine **-i** or **-é**	▶ feminine **-ie** or **ée** (no difference in pronunciation)
masculine **-e**	▶ feminine **-e** (no change)

Bon à savoir !

Some feminine forms are irregular, but they are very common.

m. -eur, f. -euse
un voleur, une voleuse
– *a (male) thief, a (female) thief*

m. -teur, f. -trice
un auditeur, une auditrice – *a listener (m. and f.)*

m. -(i)er, f. -(i)ère
un étranger, une étrangère – *a foreigner (m. and f.)*

5

Singular and Plural: Look at the pairs of words and try to determine why the second word is plural. Then read the applicable rule and pronounce the words aloud; you can hear them on the CD.

1. un ami / des amis – un bar / des bars –
   un restaurant / des restaurants – une Portugaise / des Portugaises
2. un Français / des Français – un jus / des jus – un prix / des prix
3. un animal / des animaux – un bureau / des bureaux –
   un cheveu / des cheveux

1. General plural formation: with **des / les** and the ending **-s**, which is not pronounced
2. With words that end in **-s** or **-x** in the singular: plural formation with only the plural determiner **des / les**; same form as in the singular
3. Irregular plural formation: words ending in **-a(i)l**, **-eu**, **-(e)au** end in **-aux** or **-eux** in the plural.

Bon à savoir !

The following nouns exist only in the plural:
les lunettes –
the glasses
les toilettes –
the toilet

6

Now you are in the Café Rose.
Read the following words and write the appropriate plural forms in the blanks.

1. une table _____   5. une personne _____

2. un pastis _____   6. un gâteau _____

3. une quiche _____   7. un café _____

4. un euro _____   8. une bière _____

7

Marie doesn't arrive alone.
Read the dialogue between Mounir, Marie, and Susan and mark in the text the places, nationalities, and professions. You can also listen to the dialogue on the CD.

Mounir:	Salut Marie!
Marie:	Salut Mounir! Je te présente Susan, c'est une Anglaise, elle vient de Londres.
Mounir:	Enchanté, Susan! Tu passes tes vacances à Paris?
Susan:	Non, j'habite ici. Je suis journaliste.
Marie:	Elle travaille pour Le Monde! Elle est journaliste, comme moi!
Mounir:	Oh, c'est intéressant! Et tu parles super bien français!
Susan:	Euh, je ne sais pas...
Marie:	Mais si!
Susan:	Et toi, Mounir, tu es Français?
Mounir:	Mes parents viennent du Maroc et je suis né à Casablanca. Mais j'habite en France depuis longtemps.
Susan:	Donc toi aussi, tu es bilingue, tu parles français et arabe!
Mounir:	Oui, mais tu sais, tous les Marocains sont bilingues.
Susan:	Et qu'est-ce que tu fais dans la vie?
Mounir:	Je suis étudiant. Et je travaille aussi deux jours par semaine comme vendeur dans un magasin de chaussures. Tu as besoin de chaussures?
Susan:	Pourquoi? Tu n'aimes pas mes chaussures?
Mounir:	Mais si!

> **Bon à savoir !**
> You can use the question **Qu'est-ce que vous faites dans la vie?** (*What do you do in life?*) to ask people about their profession, not life in general.

8

Search in the mix of letters for the French translations of the terms and underline them.

saleslady	dnebvendeusesi	*professor*	pprofesseureest
waiter	hseserveursesjd	*actress*	actriceuracteusah
doctor	croadocteurceds	*employee*	unenemployés

9 🖉

Professional Titles: Many French professional titles have a masculine and a feminine form. The two are distinguished from one another by their ending, like other nouns.

Which profession could Caroline and Pierre follow? Write them in the boxes.

Caroline: "Je suis…"	Pierre: "Je suis…"

> boulanger – musicienne – employé – employée – acteur –
> danseuse – actrice – boulangère – photographe – musicien –
> photographe – dentiste – danseur – dentiste

Some professional titles have just one masculine form that is used for people of either sex. These are activities that formerly were the exclusive province of men, for example, **médecin**, **docteur**, **ingénieur**, **professeur**.

10 🖉

What do these people do for a living? Write the appropriate professional title in the blanks under the pictures.

_____ _____ _____ _____

_____ _____

> a. une jardinière – b. un architecte – c. des musiciens – d. un coiffeur –
> e. une photographe – f. des joueuses de tennis

11 🖊

Look at the illustrations. How would these people introduce themselves if they were asked about their professions?

Je suis...

1. _____ 2. _____ 3. _____ 4. _____

5. _____ 6. _____ 7. _____ 8. _____

12 🖊

Bon à savoir !
The following words are not proper names, and yet they are written with a capital letter:
Pâques – *Easter*
Noël – *Christmas*
le Français –
the Frenchman

When are capital letters used? With a few exceptions, in French only proper names begin with capital letters. Names of people and cities are used without an article. Read the following sentences and check off the proper names.

> Je te présente Susan. Elle vient de Londres.
> Je m'appelle Mounir Belaoui. J'habite à Paris. Mes parents viennent du Maroc et je suis né à Casablanca. Mais j'habite en France depuis longtemps.

But with geographical names, the proper name is preceded by the definite article.

Names of continents: **l'Europe, l'Asie**...
Country names: **le Maroc, la France, les Etats-Unis**...
Names of regions, mountains, and rivers: **la Normandie, les Alpes, la Seine**...
Names of islands: **la Corse, l'île de Ré**...

In direct address the words **Monsieur** *(sir, Mr.)*, **Madame** *(madame, Mrs.)*, and **Mademoiselle** *(miss)* are used.

13 TR. 05

What is the nationality of these people? Look at the flags and write the nationality in the blanks. If you don't know the nationalities, you will find some help below. You can also listen to the sentences on the CD.

Jane vient de New York, c'est une _____ .

Caroline vient de Zurich, c'est une _____ .

Pablo vient de Madrid, c'est un _____ .

Laura et Teresa viennent de Rome,

ce sont des _____ .

Les parents de Mounir viennent de Casablanca.

Ce sont des _____ .

les Etats-Unis – *the USA* – **l'Américain/e** – *the American*
la Suisse – *Switzerland* – **le/la Suisse** – *the Swiss (m. and f.)*
l'Espagne – *Spain* – **l'Espagnol/e** – *the Spaniard (m. and f.)*
l'Italie – *Italy* – **l'Italien/ne** – *the Italian (m. and f.)*
le Maroc – *Morocco* – **le/la Marocain/e** – *the Moroccan (m. and f.)*

14 ✎

Look at the following groups of words. One word with a different gender has slipped into each group—that is, it's the only one that is either masculine or feminine. But be careful! The nouns may also be in the plural.

1. v**in**
   - ▢ a. pa**in**
   - ▢ b. from**age**
   - ▢ c. bagu**ette**

2. pomm**es**
   - ▢ a. orang**es**
   - ▢ b. anan**as**
   - ▢ c. banan**es**

3. vél**os**
   - ▢ a. voit**ures**
   - ▢ b. tra**ins**
   - ▢ c. bat**eaux**

4. mant**eau**
   - ▢ a. rob**e**
   - ▢ b. chem**ise**
   - ▢ c. chauss**ure**

5. chi**enne**
   - ▢ a. Parisi**enne**
   - ▢ b. ch**atte**
   - ▢ c. dent**iste**

6. journal**isme**
   - ▢ a. journal
   - ▢ b. entrepr**ise**
   - ▢ c. employ**é**

15 ✎

Connect the countries and nationalities on the left with the English translations on the right.

le Chinois le Mexicain
l'Algérien le Belge
le Russe

1. le Chinois	a. *the Mexican woman*
2. l'Algérie	b. *Russia*
3. les Belges	c. *the Algerian woman*
4. la Russie	d. *the Chinese*
5. l'Algérienne	e. *Mexico*
6. la Mexicaine	f. *the Arab*
7. le Mexique	g. *Algeria*
8. l'arabe	h. *the Belgians*

Masculine—Feminine/Professions

1

Write the feminine forms of the terms in the blanks.

1. un ami _____

2. un employé _____

3. un professeur _____

4. un photographe _____

5. un musicien _____

2

Look at the columns of terms. Only one term is appropriate to each illustration.

☐ a. un étudiant   ☐ a. un médecin   ☐ a. une cuisinière
☐ b. des étudiants   ☐ b. une femme médecin   ☐ b. un cuisinier
☐ c. une étudiante   ☐ c. des médecins   ☐ c. un jardinier

☐ a. des Chinoises   ☐ a. des serveurs   ☐ a. un photographe
☐ b. des Portugaises   ☐ b. une serveuse   ☐ b. une photographe
☐ c. des Anglaises   ☐ c. un serveur   ☐ c. des photographes

Singular—Plural/Professions

3 🖉

Write the plural forms of the terms in the blanks.

1. animal   _____

2. bureau   _____

3. bar   _____

4. Anglais   _____

5. Portugaise   _____

6. joueur de tennis   _____

4 🖉

Find the word that doesn't match the topic of the other words. The questions may help you.

1. Which word does not refer to a country?
   - a. la France
   - b. la Seine
   - c. la Chine
   - d. la Belgique

2. Which word is not a general form of address?
   - a. Monsieur
   - b. Mademoiselle
   - c. Mounir
   - d. Madame

3. Which word does not refer to a profession?
   - a. une musicienne
   - b. une Parisienne
   - c. une professeur
   - d. une danseuse

4. Which word does not refer to a country?
   - a. le Maroc
   - b. la Belgique
   - c. les Etats-Unis
   - d. les Alpes

1

Read the sentences in which various forms of the verb **être** are hidden.
Match the sentences with the appropriate illustrations. You can also listen
to the sentences on the CD.

1. _____ 2. _____ 3. _____

4. _____ 5. _____ 6. _____

> a. Vous êtes Monsieur…? b. Tu es gentil! c. Elle est fatiguée.
> d. Ils sont journalistes e. Je suis Mounir f. Nous sommes joyeux!

2

Here you can read what various people like to do in their free time. You will
see the forms of the verb **aimer** (*to like*) for the various persons. A verb
in the basic form (the infinitive) is always used after the verb **aimer**; it
specifies what the person likes to do.

1. J'aim**e** nager.
2. Tu aim**es** faire du ski.
3. Elle aim**e** danser.
4. Nous aim**ons** jouer du piano.
5. Vous aim**ez** aller au cinéma.
6. Ils aim**ent** jouer au tennis.

3 TR. 07

With the help of the illustration on the right, try to find the right verb forms. Write them in the blanks. You can also listen to the verb forms on the CD.

1. Je _____ Marie.

2. Tu _____ gentil.

3. Nous _____ médecins.

je suis	nous sommes
tu es	vous êtes
il est	ils sont

The verb **être** is used
• generally to designate a person: **Je suis Mounir.**
• for an internal or external description: **Pierre est fatigué/ beau.**
• to specify origin: **Tu es Français.**
• to specify profession: **Ils sont journalistes.**
• to specify civil state: **Nous sommes mariés** *(married)*.
• to specify time of day: **Il est deux heures/midi.**

4 TR. 08

The verb **avoir** is irregular. Look at the illustration at the right and complete the following sentences using the correct verb forms. You can also listen to the verb forms on the CD.

1. Pierre et Caroline *a / ont / avons*
   faim.

2. S'il vous plaît, Monsieur, est-ce
   que vous *a / ont / avez* l'heure?

3. Catherine et moi,
   nous *a / avons / as* trente ans.

The verb **avoir** is used
• in referring to property: **J'ai un chien.**
• to specify belonging: **Ils ont deux enfants.**
• to express how a person feels: **Vous avez faim/froid?**
• to specify one's age: **Tu as quel âge? J'ai trente ans.**

5

Which of these words are forms of **être**, and which are forms of **avoir**?
Fill in the blanks.

être: _____

avoir: _____

> es – avons – as – est – sommes – suis – ont – êtes – sont – ai

Bon à savoir !

C'est / ce sont are
used to name or
describe something or
introduce someone:
C'est beau!
That's beautiful!
C'est un chien.
That is a dog.
C'est Caroline.
That is Caroline.
**Ce sont mes
chaussures.**
Those are my shoes.

6 [TR. 09]

Verbs in the Present Tense:
In French there are three regular verb groups. A verb consists of a word
stem and an ending.

The verbs of the first group end in **-er**; the verbs of the second group end
in **-ir**:

> **parler** – stem **parl-** + ending **-er**,
> **finir** – stem **fin-** + ending **-ir**.

Look at the conjugations of both verb groups in the chart (you can also
listen to them on the CD) and conjugate the verbs provided below along
the same pattern.
Note that with the second-group verbs (**-ir**), there is a **-ss-** between the
stem and the ending in the three plural forms.

Bon à savoir !

Many French verbs
belong in the first
group (**-er**).

A few other common
verbs from the second
group are **agir** – *to act*,
choisir – *to choose*,
grandir – *to grow*,
réfléchir – *to reflect*,
réussir – *to succeed*.

je	parl – **e**
tu	parl – **es**
il/elle	parl – **e**
nous	parl – **ons**
vous	parl – **ez**
ils/elles	parl – **ent**

danser *(to dance)*: _____

je	fini – **s**
tu	fini – **s**
il/elle	fini – **t**
nous	fini – **ss** – **ons**
vous	fini – **ss** – **ez**
ils/elles	fini – **ss** – **ent**

choisir *(to choose)*: _____

7 🖉

Here you can see what various people do after work. Read the statements / questions below and match them up with the correct pictures. Pay attention to the verb forms.

1. _____ 2. _____ 3. _____

4. _____ 5. _____ 6. _____

> a. elle joue du violon   b. vous restez à la maison?
> c. ils écoutent de la musique   d. nous jouons au tennis
> e. je réfléchis   f. tu regardes la télé?

8 TR. 10

Marie, Mounir, and Susan are hungry. They first consider where they want to go, and later on, once they have arrived at the restaurant, everyone orders something. Read both dialogues; you can also listen to them on the CD.

Marie:	Il est 13 heures. J'ai faim, et vous?
Mounir:	Oui, nous aussi, nous avons faim.
Marie:	Vous aimez la cuisine chinoise?
Susan:	Oh oui, moi, j'aime beaucoup manger chinois!
Marie:	Il y a un restaurant tout près d'ici…

Le serveur:	Bonjour, qu'est-ce que vous mangez?
Marie:	Je choisis le plat du jour, le poulet au basilic.
Susan:	Euh … Nous réfléchissons encore…
Le serveur:	Réfléchissez tranquillement, vous avez le temps!
Marie:	Oh non, il faut choisir vite, s'il vous plaît! J'ai faim, moi!

9

Among the first-group verbs there are a few that have regular endings but peculiarities in the stem.

- Verbs ending in **-eter**, **-ener**, **-ever**, **-érer**, such as **acheter** (*to buy*) (see chart), **amener** (*to bring*), **emmener** (*to take*), **lever** (*to lift*), **préférer** (*to prefer*), and **espérer** (*to hope*), change in spelling and pronunciation.
- Verbs ending in **-eler**, such as **appeler** (*to call*) (see chart): an **e** is audible only in the third person plural.

j'	achète	j'	appelle
tu	achètes	tu	appelles
il/elle/on	achète	il/elle/on	appelle
nous	achetons	nous	appelons
vous	achetez	vous	appelez
ils/elles	achètent	ils/elles	appellent

You can also listen to the conjugation on the CD.

- Verbs ending in **-ger** and **-cer**, such as **manger**, **bouger** (*to move*), **nager**, **changer**, **échanger** (*to exchange*), **commencer** (*to begin*), and **avancer** (*to advance*): the first person plural changes by adding an **e** or a **ç cédille**. The pronunciation doesn't change, however.
- **je mange – nous mangeons / je commence – nous commençons**

> **Bon à savoir !**
>
> The **cédille** is a special pronunciation symbol in French. Its effect is to soften a **c** so that it's pronounced like an **s** before the vowels **a**, **o**, and **u**, as in **français**.

10

Put the verb forms in order according to the conjugation pattern, following the sequence **je/tu/il/nous/vous/ils**.

1. sommes – suis – sont – êtes – est – es

_____

2. ai – as – a – avons – avez – ont

_____

3. pense – penses – pense – pensez – pensons – pensent

_____

4. agis – agit – agis – agissent – agissez – agissons

_____

11 ✏️

The spaces have been left out of these sentences. Write the words separately.

1. Ilestdeuxheures. _____

2. Lesenfantsontdeuxans. _____

3. Ilsnagentbien. _____

4. Nousaimonsskier. _____

5. Nouscommençonslefrançais. _____

6. Nouschoisissonsunplat. _____

7. Tuachètesunvélo. _____

8. Vousachetezdesgâteaux. _____

12 🎧 TR. 12

In French, several verb forms sound the same or similar, for in the spoken language the endings are indistinguishable. In this case the spelling can be deduced only from the context. Look at the sentences and choose the correct verb form. You can also listen to the individual sentences on the CD.

1. Mon oncle et ma tante *habitent / habites / habite* à Paris.

2. Ma tante *s'appellent / s'appelle / s'appeler* Fatiha,

   elle *parle / parles / parlent* français et arabe.

3. Elle *sont / a / avez* un petit chien. Il *s'appellent / s'appelle / s'appeler*

   Gaston.

4. C'*a / ai / est* un caniche.

5. Thierry, *c'es / est / êtes* mon oncle.

6. Je l'*aime / aiment / aimes* vraiment bien.

7. Il *aime / aimez / aimes* le vin et il *mange / manges / mangent* souvent

   dans un restaurant.

8. Mais à Paris, il y *a / es / sont* beaucoup de restaurants, il faut *choisir /*

   choisis / choisissent!

13 🖉

Look at the pictures and choose the appropriate description; check off the correct answer.

1. ▨ a. elle danse
   ▨ b. il mange
   ▨ c. elle mange

2. ▨ a. ils travaillent
   ▨ b. ils nagent
   ▨ c. nous nageons

3. ▨ a. ils jouent
   ▨ b. elles jouent
   ▨ c. elle joue

4. ▨ a. elle finit
   ▨ b. elle réfléchit
   ▨ c. elle joue

5. ▨ a. il neige
   ▨ b. le soleil brille
   ▨ c. ils skient

6. ▨ a. ce sont des piscines
   ▨ b. c'est une piscine
   ▨ c. sept une piscine

14 🖉

Ce soir means *this evening*. Here you can see what people have planned. Write the corresponding verb forms in the present tense in the blanks.

1. Ce soir, nous (manger) _____ chinois, nous (avoir)

   _____ déjà faim!

2. Ce soir, il faut (emmener) _____ un manteau, tu (avoir)

   _____ toujours froid.

3. Ce soir, je (rester) _____ à la maison, j'(avoir) _____

   mal à la tête.

4. Ce soir, ils (regarder) _____ la télé, il y (avoir) _____

   un bon film.

5. Ce soir, nous (nager) _____ dans la piscine, c'(être)

   _____ l'été!

15 🖉

Here are some well-known French sayings—but the verbs are missing.
The basic forms are provided; write the appropriate verb forms in
the blanks.

Translations of the ▶
popular sayings:
1. *I think, therefore
   I am.*
2. *When the cat's
   away, the mice
   will play.*
3. *At night all cats are
   gray: at night it's
   impossible to dis-
   tinguish people and
   things clearly.*
4. *You eat enough for
   four.*
5. *He's in the clouds: he
   can't keep his mind
   on things.*

1. Je (penser) _____ donc je (être) _____ .

2. Quand le chat (être) _____ sorti, les souris (danser) _____ .

3. La nuit, tous les chats (être) _____ gris.

4. Tu (manger) _____ comme quatre.

5. Il (être) _____ dans les nuages.

16 🖉

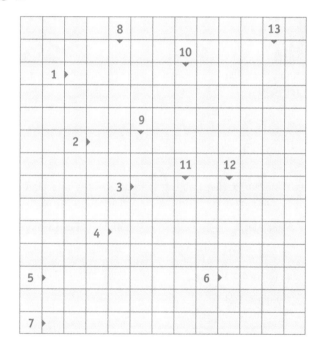

Horizontal:
1. penser (tu)
2. finir (nous)
3. grandir (je / tu)
4. commencer (vous)
5. avoir (nous)
6. être (il, elle, on)
7. appeler (ils, elles)

Vertical:
8. avoir (ils, elles)
9. nager (nous)
10. être (je)
11. aimer (je / il, elle, on)
12. donner (ils, elles)
13. choisir (ils, elles)

1

Complete these sentences with forms of the verb **être** or **avoir**. The basic forms are provided in parentheses at the end of each sentence.

1. Susan _____ journaliste. (être)

2. Elle _____ trente ans. (avoir)

3. Vous _____ le chef! (être)

4. Vous _____ faim? (avoir)

5. Il y _____ un gâteau sur la table de la cuisine. (avoir)

6. Ce _____ mes chaussures. (être)

7. C' _____ la phrase numéro sept! (être)

2

Which sentences match the illustrations? Check off the correct box.

1. ▓ a. Il a faim.   2. ▓ a. Nous avons un chien.
   ▓ b. Ils ont faim.   ▓ b. Nous sommes Autrichiens.
   ▓ c. Elles ont faim.   ▓ c. Vous êtes Autrichiens.

3. ▓ a. Elle est   4. ▓ a. Il est minuit.   5. ▓ a. Il y a des oranges.
       fatiguée.   ▓ b. Il a une amie.   ▓ b. Elle a des oranges.
   ▓ b. Il est fatigué.   ▓ c. Il est midi.   ▓ c. Il a deux oranges.
   ▓ c. Elles sont
       fatiguées.

3 ✏

Complete these sentences with the appropriate forms of **danser** (*to dance*) and **finir** (*to finish*).

1. Nous aimons _____ .

2. On _____ le travail dans la semaine.

3. Thomas et Sophie _____ de manger.

4. Mes parents _____ bien.

5. Moi, je _____ mal.

6. Il faut _____ la leçon.

4 ✏

Choose the verb form that fits in each sentence.

1. Mon oncle et ma tante *habitent / habites / habite* à Paris.
2. Ils *on / ont / sont* une fille de 30 ans.
3. Elle *s'appellent / s'appelle / s'appeler* Charlotte.
4. C'est / es / ai ma cousine.
5. Pierre *ai / es / est* mon cousin.
6. Je l'*aime / aiment / aimes* vraiment bien.

5 ✏

Change these sentences to the plural (**je** becomes **nous**, **tu** changes to **vous**, **il / elle** change to **ils / elles**).

1. Ce soir, je mange dans un restaurant. (nous)

_____

2. Tu achètes beaucoup de CDs. (vous)

_____

3. Elle appelle Pierre. (elles)

_____

4. C'est un journaliste, il commence le travail. (ils)

_____

5. Je commence le français. (nous)

_____

1 TR. 13

Madame Duval has plans to go into town today. Before leaving she considers what she will need and where she has to go. Fill in the blanks with the appropriate words. You can also listen to the sentences on the CD.

1. D'abord, je vais chez le boulanger. Là, j'achète un _____ .

2. Puis, je vais à la poste. A la poste, j'achète des _____ pour

   poster une _____ .

3. Après, je vais à la banque. Mais il me faut aussi des _____ !

4. Je vais dans tous les _____ !

> a. pain   b. lettre   c. timbres   d. magasins   e. chaussures

2 TR. 14

Now she is in the supermarket. Read what she needs and match up her statements with the appropriate pictures. You can also listen to the sentences on the CD.

1. _____   2. _____   3. _____   4. _____

5. _____   6. _____   7. _____   8. _____

> a. du dentifrice   b. de la limonade   c. des pommes   d. du café
> e. un kilo de sucre   f. de l'eau   g. un paquet de thé   h. des oranges

The Definite Article

3

The definite article is used to clearly designate specific or generally known things or persons.

Forms:

Singular	masculine	**le**	**le soleil**, **le timbre**, **le monsieur**
	feminine	**la**	**la lune**, **la dame**, **la boulangerie**
Plural		**les**	**les banques**, **les magasins**, **les hôtels**

Before vowels (**a**, **e**, **i**, **o**, **u**, **y**) and a mute **h**, **le** and **la** are shortened to **l'** (spoken as "lapostrophe"): **l'amour** (m.), **l'eau** (f.), **l'homme** (m.).

Choose the correct article:

1. *le / la / l'* banque (f)
2. *le / la / l'* magasin (m)
3. *le / la / l'* eau (f)
4. *le / la / les* banques (pl)

4

Now it's your turn. Where do people go and what can they buy when they have to go shopping? Write the word with the definite articles **le – la – l' – les** in the blanks under each picture.

1. _____ 2. _____ 3. _____ 4. _____ 5. _____

_____ _____ _____ _____ _____

6. _____ 7. _____ 8. _____ 9. _____ 10. _____

_____ _____ _____ _____ _____

5

Fill in the blanks with **le – la – l' – les**!

1. _____ matin, Madame Duval fait _____ courses.

2. Elle va à _____ banque, à _____ poste, à _____ épicerie.

3. Elle va dans _____ magasins du quartier.

In French the definite article is always used

- before place names: names of countries (**le Canada**, **la Chine**, **l'Espagne**), continents (**l'Europe**, **l'Asie**, departments, provinces, fairly large islands (**les Ardennes**, **la Normandie**, **la Corse**).
- after the verbs **aimer**, **adorer**, **détester**, and **préférer**: **J'aime le fromage. Je déteste les mathématiques.**

> **Bon à savoir !**
>
> When the definite article is used before a time of day, it means that the action is repetitive.
> **Le matin, Madame Duval fait les courses.**
> *In the morning Mrs. Duval goes shopping.*
> **Le samedi, elle mange souvent au restaurant.**
> *On Saturdays she often eats in the restaurant.*

6 TR. 15

Mounir and Marie have an appointment. Mounir arrives late. Read the dialogue and check off the indefinite articles **un – une – des**! You can also listen to the dialogue on the CD.

Mounir: Salut, Marie…

Marie: Salut, Mounir, tu as une montre? Il est déjà dix heures!

Mounir: Oui, je suis désolé, mais un voisin … et puis le facteur…

Marie: Oui, oui, tu trouves toujours des excuses! Bon, on prend le prochain métro? Tu as un billet?

Mounir: Oui, j'ai un billet, mais j'ai aussi faim … je m'achète un petit pain au chocolat!

Marie: Ah, le petit-déjeuner! Bon d'accord mais vite, le métro part dans cinq minutes.

Mounir: Pas de problème, il y a une boulangerie juste là.

Mounir: Bonjour, je voudrais un petit pain au chocolat.

Le boulanger: Désolé, il n'y en a plus! Mais il y a des croissants, et aussi des sandwiches…

Mounir: Bon, alors, je voudrais un croissant! Et une bouteille de jus d'orange, s'il vous plaît!

Marie: Vite, Mounir, il nous reste encore une minute!

Mounir: Une minute pour le petit-déjeuner, ça va!

3

Indefinite Articles—Partitive Articles

7

The indefinite article is used to designate persons and things that are not explained further.

Forms:
Singular   masculine   **un**   un ananas
            feminine   **une**   une pomme
Plural   **des**   des oranges

In English there is no exact correspondence with this use of the indefinite article.

Je mange des oranges. *I eat (some) oranges.*

8 TR. 16

The use of the partitive article is distinguished from the indefinite article by referring to an unspecified part of a quantity that is uncountable or abstract.

Forms:
Singular   masculine   **du**   du sucre, du fromage
            feminine   **de la**   de la farine, de la chance

However, if this part of an uncountable quantity is clarified by the addition of a specification of quantity, the article disappears and only the preposition **de** (or **d'** before a vowel) is retained.

J'achète 500 grammes de fromage et une bouteille de vin.
Il a beaucoup de chance.
Il y a une bouteille d'eau dans le frigidaire.

Look at the pictures on the right and complete the following sentences with the correct articles. You can also listen to the sentences on the CD.

1. J'achète _____ pomme.

2. Il y a _____ farine sur la table.

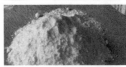

3. Ce sont 50 grammes _____ beurre.

9 ✎

When Mr. Dupont is away, it's a really special trip. Write the appropriate definite or indefinite articles in the blanks.

1. Monsieur Dupont habite sur _____ Côte d'Azur.

2. Il travaille dans _____ restaurant, comme chef cuisinier.

3. _____ été, il y a beaucoup de touristes – et beaucoup de travail!

4. Mais pour lui, _____ cuisine est déjà _____ voyage!

5. Il a _____ recettes françaises mais il aime aussi beaucoup _____
   cuisines du monde.

6. Chaque jour, il y a _____ autre pays "à la carte". Le lundi, c'est _____
   Chine, _____ mardi, _____ Espagne...

un – la – L' – un –
la – des – un – les –
le – la – l'

10 ✎

Madame Duval has written a letter to a friend and brings it to the post office. Unfortunately, she has forgotten both the address and her glasses. And to make matters worse, all the articles have disappeared from the dialogue.

Mme Duval: Bonjour, je voudrais poster _____ lettre.

L'employée des postes: Oui, Madame. C'est _____ lettre pour _____
France?

Mme Duval: Non, pour _____ Etats-Unis!

L'employée des postes: Et quelle est _____ destination précise?

Mme Duval: C'est _____ lettre à _____ amie!

L'employée des postes: D'accord, mais il manque _____ adresse! Il faut
marquer _____ nom, _____ ville et _____ pays sur _____ enveloppe!

Mme Duval: Ah oui, c'est vrai, excusez-moi! Vous avez _____ stylo? Merci!
Oh non! Où sont mes lunettes?

L'employée des postes: J'ai _____ idée, Madame. Vous me donnez _____
coordonnées et j'écris _____ adresse sur _____ enveloppe pour vous. Et
voici _____ timbre pour _____ Etats-Unis!

Mme Duval: Alors maintenant on a tout _____ adresse et _____ timbre.

Bon à savoir !

What you write on
a letter are **les
coordonnées**—*personal
data*. This refers to
name, address, phone
number, and e-mail
address.

11

Mme Duval goes to the bank to take out some money because she wants to buy some shoes. Read the dialogue and fill in the blanks with the proper articles. You can also listen to the dialogue on the CD.

1. **Mme Duval:** Bonjour, je voudrais acheter _____ chaussures.

2. **Employé:** Je sui désolé, Madame, mais ici, c'est _____ banque et non pas un magasin de chaussures!

3. **Mme Duval:** Oui, bien sûr, jeune homme, mais il me faut _____ l'argent pour acheter les chaussures, n'est-ce pas?

4. **Employé:** Ah, d'accord, vous voulez retirer _____ somme de votre compte!

5. **Mme Duval:** Oui, j'ai _____ compte ici.

6. **Employé:** Bon, alors, il faut _____ nom et _____ numéro de compte.

7. **Mme Duval:** D'accord, je m'appelle Francine Duval et le numéro de compte, c'est ... c'est ... hmm ... ah voilà, j'ai _____ carte de crédit. Mais quel est le numéro ... Où sont mes lunettes ... Ah, _____ lunettes, je cherche toujours les lunettes ...

8. **Employé:** Donnez-moi _____ carte, Madame, c'est mieux.

9. **Mme Duval:** Ah, très bien, merci, vous êtes vraiment _____ personne très aimable. Vous voulez _____ chocolat?

10. **Employé:** Oui, merci, pourquoi pas, j'aime _____ chocolat!

12

You are in the plane and the flight attendant offers you something. Fill in the blanks in your answers with the terms suggested below.

a. une bouteille
b. un verre
c. un peu

1. Vous voulez de la limonade? Non, merci, je voudrais _____ de jus de fruits.

2. Vous voulez de l'eau gazeuse? Non, merci, je préfère _____ d'eau plate.

3. Vous voulez du thé? Non, merci, pour moi, _____ de café.

13 ✎

Here is the recipe for making crêpes. Check off the correct articles.

Pour (1) *une / un / la* pâte à crêpes, il faut (2) *la / de la / de l'*
farine, (3) *de / le / du* lait, deux œufs, 10 grammes (4) *des / de /*
du beurre et un peu (5) *des / de / du* sel. On mélange (6) *les / la /*
du farine et (7) *la / de la / les* œufs. Puis on ajoute (8) *les / le /*
le autres ingrédients. (9) *Le / De la / La* pâte est prête! On prépare
(10) *le / les / de* crêpes à la poêle. Bon appétit!

14 ✎

Write the partitive articles in the blanks after the expressions of quantity.
Where there is no information before the blanks, the quantities are
unspecified.

1. 200 grammes _____
   beurre

2. beaucoup _____
   sucre

3. _____ farine

4. un peu _____ sel

5. _____ œufs

15 🖉

Which picture goes with which quantity? Write the quantities under the pictures.

1. _____ 2. _____ 3. _____ 4. _____

5. _____ 6. _____ 7. _____ 8. _____

9. _____ 10. _____ 11. _____ 12. _____

> a. du café   b. un paquet de café   c. une tasse de café
> d. une cuillère de café   e. du beurre   f. un verre de bière
> g. deux cafés   h. un verre de vin   i. une baguette
> j. des baguettes   k. du vin   l. de la baguette

1 ✎

Look at the pictures and write the appropriate terms in the blanks.

1. _____   2. _____   3. _____

4. _____   5. _____   6. _____

> a. la poste   b. un supermarché   c. l'eau
> d. le journal   e. une épicerie   f. des lettres

2 ✎

Complete the sentences with **le / la / l' / les** or **un / une / des**.

1. Madame Duval est _____ personne aimable.

2. Elle voudrait poster _____ lettre à _____ amie.

3. Elle aime acheter _____ chaussures.

4. Et elle a toujours _____ bonbons pour _____ employés.

5. Mais elle cherche toujours _____ lunettes dans son sac.

3 🖉

Write the missing definite or indefinite articles in the blanks.

1. ● Bonjour, est-ce que vous avez _____ pommes?

2. ○ Bien sûr! J'ai _____ pommes italiennes, _____ pommes françaises...

3. ● Ah, j'aime bien _____ pommes italiennes! _____ kilo, s'il vous plaît...

4. ○ Bien. Et avec ça? _____ bananes? _____ oranges?

5. ● Non, merci, je n'aime pas _____ oranges, mais je voudrais _____ ananas ...

4 🖉

Read the terms and check off the corresponding picture.

	a.	b.	c.
1. une baguette			
2. un peu de vin			
3. des fromages		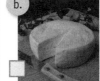	
4. 50 grammes de farine			

1

Madame Colin wants to fly away for a vacation. She packs her suitcase. Read what she takes, paying attention to the adjectives **ce – cette – cet – ces**. They refer to items that Mme Colin has selected. You can also listen to the sentences on the CD.

1. J'emmène ce maillot de bain.
2. J'emmène ce pantalon.
3. J'emmène cette robe.
4. J'emmène cet appareil photo.
5. J'emmène ces tee-shirts.
6. J'emmène ces lunettes de soleil.

2

Look at Mounir in his room. He wants to go on vacation with his aunt, but he has overslept. He has only a half hour to pack his things. Marie picks him up and helps him search. Connect the correct answers from Marie with his questions.

a. Ta chemise est sur le sol.

1. Où est mon maillot de bain?

b. Ton pull est juste là!

2. Où est ma chemise?

c. Ta crème solaire est sous la chaise.

3. Où sont mes livres?

d. Tes livres sont sur la commode.

4. Où est mon pull?

e. Ton maillot de bain est sur le lit.

5. Où est ma crème solaire?

Demonstrative adjectives

For emphasis, and especially in the spoken language, a **-là** is often attached to the noun.

Je préfère ce pantalon-là. *I prefer those pants (there).*

3

Fill in the following blanks using the chart.

1. J'emmène _____ tee-shirt.

2. J'emmène _____ chemise.

ce t-shirt	
cette chemise	
cet appareil	
ces chaussures	

The demonstrative adjective refers to a specific person or thing that is located near the speaker or that was recently mentioned.

Singular   masculine **ce**
　　　　masculine **cet** (before a vowel or a mute **h**)
　　　　feminine **cette**
Plural　　　**ces**

Read aloud the following examples:

1. **Ce train va à Marseille.** *This train goes to Marseilles.*
2. **Cet appareil photo est pratique.** *This camera is practical.*
3. **Cette route mène à la mer.** *This road goes to the sea.*
4. **J'aime ces chaussures.** *I like these shoes.*

4 TR. 19

Read the dialogue in the travel agency and choose the missing appropriate demonstrative adjectives. You can also listen to the dialogue on the CD.

Client: Bonjour, je voudrais prendre un avion pour Nice mardi matin.

ces
cet
ce
ce
cette
ce

1. **Employé:** _____ avion est presque complet! Mais il y a encore des places en "classe affaires".

2. **Client:** Ah, mais _____ places sont chères. Est-ce qu'il y a un vol mardi après-midi?

3. **Employé:** Oui. Et pour _____ vol, j'ai encore des places économiques!

4. **Client:** Bon, alors, je préfère _____ solution!

　Employé: Et le retour?

5. **Client:** Pour _____ mercredi, s'il vous plaît.

6. **Employé:** Ah! Dans _____ cas, il y a une offre: moins 30% pour les aller-retours en deux jours.

　Client: C'est parfait!

5 ✏

This flight and no other! Sometimes you want a very specific flight or seat. Write the appropriate demonstrative adjectives before the words.

1. _____ avion

2. _____ place

3. _____ vol

4. _____ classe

5. _____ pilote

6. _____ ligne

7. _____ billet

8. _____ airbus

6

Read the examples of various times. What is the difference in use between the definite articles **le – la – l' – les** and the demonstrative adjectives **ce – cette – cet – ces**? You can also listen to the sentences on the CD.

Le matin, Mounir est fatigué. – Ce matin, Mounir part en vacances!
Le samedi, il travaille. – Ce samedi, il va à la plage.

We already know **le matin** (*in the morning*) and **le samedi** (*on Saturdays*). The definite article before an expression of time means that the action is one that's repeated.

When a demonstrative adjective comes before an expression of time, a part of the current year or day is indicated.

ce matin (*this morning*) – **cette année** (*this year*) – **cet après-midi** (*this afternoon*) – **ce soir** (*tonight*) – **ce samedi** (*this Saturday*)

Demonstrative Adjectives

7 🖉

Look at the French sentences and choose the correct translation.

1. Le soir, je ne travaille pas.

- a. I'm not working tonight.
- b. I don't work evenings.
- c. I'm not working that night.

2. Ce soir, il va au restaurant.

- a. Tonight he's going to the restaurant.
- b. He goes to the restaurant at night.
- c. He's going to the restaurant that evening.

3. Cet été, nous nageons tous les jours.

- a. We swim all day long in the summer.
- b. It's summer! We swim all day!
- c. This summer we swim every day.

4. Cette année, nous restons à la maison.

- a. We stay home every year.
- b. Next year we will stay home.
- c. This year we're staying home.

5. Le samedi, on ne travaille pas.

- a. We don't work on Saturdays.
- b. We're not working next Saturday.
- c. We're not working this Saturday.

6. Ce matin, Mounir part en vacances.

- a. This morning Mounir is leaving for vacation.
- b. Mounir leaves for vacation tomorrow.
- c. Every morning Mounir leaves for vacation.

8 [R. 21]

Marie picks up Mounir to bring him to the airport. Before they leave, she checks to see if he has forgotten anything. Read the dialogue and pay attention to the possessive adjectives in bold print. You can also listen to the dialogue on the CD.

Marie: Alors, Mounir, tu as tout?
Mounir: Euh, oui … J'ai **mon** maillot de bain, **mes** lunettes de soleil, **ma** crème solaire…
Marie: Et **tes** affaires de toilette?
Mounir: Oui! **Mon** shampoing, **ma** brosse à dents, **mon** dentifrice…
Marie: Et là, sur la table, **ton** appareil photo!
Mounir: Non, je le laisse ici, Fatiha emmène **son** appareil et Thierry **sa** caméra!
Marie: Bon … et tu as les billets?
Mounir: Ah, les billets … attends … Oui. Voilà **mon** billet … et voilà **leurs** billets. Ça va, je suis prêt, je ferme juste **ma** valise … Oh là là, **notre** avion part dans une heure!

Marie: Vous arrivez quand à Marseille?
Mounir: A 13 heures. Puis, on va directement à la plage!
Marie: Avec **vos** valises?!
Mounir: Mais non, bien sûr, nous emmenons **nos** affaires à l'hôtel! Bon, ça y est, **ma** valise est fermée. On y va!

Marie: Euh … excuse-moi, Mounir, mais ces chaussures-là, sous **ton** lit…
Mounir: Quoi, quelles chaussures? Oh, non, ce n'est pas vrai, **mes** chaussures!

Possessive Adjectives

9

Look at who owns the various objects. Mounir will tell you.

1. C'est sa caméra!   = la caméra de Thierry
2. C'est son appareil!   = l'appareil de Fatiha
3. Ce sont leurs billets! = les billets de Thierry et Fatiha
4. Ce sont vos valises!   = les valises de Mounir, Fatiha et Thierry

> **Bon à savoir !**
>
> Because the sex of the possessor doesn't matter in the singular, in French you can't tell the difference between
> *her parents* –
> **ses parents**
> *her dog*
> **son chien**

If there is only one possessor, the possessive adjectives are as follows:
- for one object:
  mon, **ton**, **son** with an object that has a masculine grammatical gender
  ma, **ta**, **sa** with an object that has a feminine grammatical gender
  (Before a vowel or a mute **h**, **ma**, **ta**, and **sa** change to **mon**, **ton**, and **son**.)
  mon appareil photo – ma brosse à dents – mon amie
- with multiple objects: **mes**, **tes**, **ses**
  mes billets et mes valises

When there are multiple possessors, the possessive adjectives are as follows:
- with one object: **notre**, **votre**, **leur**
  Notre train part dans 30 minutes.
- with multiple objects: **nos**, **vos**, **leurs**
  Nous laissons nos affaires à l'hôtel!

10 🖉

Here the people say what belongs to them. Change the sentences around by replacing the item in bold print with the object in parentheses. Here is an example:
C'est mon **oncle**. (tante) ▸ **C'est ma tante**.

1. C'est ma **valise**. (billet) _____

2. C'est ta **brosse à dents**. (dentifrice)_____

3. Ce sont **tes lunettes de soleil**. (chaussures)_____

4. C'est **mon avion**. (place) _____

5. C'est **son appareil-photo**. (tee-shirt) _____

11 🖉

Mounir, Fatiha, and Thierry take a few thing along on vacation. You can see precisely what these are in the illustrations. Complete the sentences with the appropriate possessive adjectives and nouns.

1. Fatiha et Thierry emmènent _____ .

2. Ils emmènent _____ .

3. Ils ont aussi _____ .

4. Le monsieur demande: "Vous avez _____ ?"

5. Fatiha: "Mounir a _____ , mais _____ part

   dans 30 minutes!"

12 🖉

Read the terms and check off the correct translations. Sometimes there are more than one correct answer. You can also listen to the terms on the CD.

1. sa voiture
- ▨ a. this car
- ▨ b. his carn
- ▨ c. her car

2. leur valise
- ▨ a. their suitcase
- ▨ b. their suitcases
- ▨ c. his suitcase

3. ses lunettes de soleil
- ▨ a. his sunglasses
- ▨ b. their sunglasses
- ▨ c. her sunglasses

4. votre appareil photo
- ▨ a. your (formal) camera
- ▨ b. our camera
- ▨ c. your (plural) camera

5. ce soir
- ▨ a. this evening
- ▨ b. tonight
- ▨ c. his evening

13 ✏️

Fatiha and Thierry, Mounir's uncle and aunt, are already at the airport.
Only Mounir is not there yet. But he has their plane tickets. Put the correct
possessive adjectives into the blanks.

1. Fatiha et Thierry sont à l'aéroport, avec _____ valises.

2. **Thierry:** Qu'est-ce qu'il fait, Mounir?_____ avion part dans une

   demi-heure!

3. **Fatiha:** Et il a _____ billets d'avion, en plus!

4. **Thierry:** Ah, le voilà! Avec _____ deux valises, c'est beaucoup pour

   une semaine!

5. **Mounir:** Salut, Thierry, salut, Fatiha! Excusez-moi de _____ retard!

6. **Fatiha:** Mais Mounir, tu emmènes toute _____ armoire?

7. **Mounir:** Mais non! C'est à cause de _____ chaussures!

14 ✏️

Write the English translations under the pictures labeled in French.

cet avion

son avion

mes lunettes de soleil

ses lunettes de soleil

1. _____ 2. _____ 3. _____ 4. _____

cette valise

sa valise

nos billets

son billet

5. _____ 6. _____ 7. _____ 8. _____

Demonstrative and Possessive Adjectives

1 🖉

Complete the sentences with the appropriate demonstrative adjectives.

1. A Marseille? Moi aussi, je prends _____ avion!

2. Vous faites souvent _____ voyage?

3. Oui! J'aime beaucoup _____ ville!

    Dans l'avion:

4. Bonjour, _____ place est libre?

5. Non, c'est la place de _____ monsieur.

6. Mais _____ deux places-là sont libres.

2 🖉

Answer the questions with "yes" and the correct possessive adjectives.

1. C'est la valise de ce monsieur?

    Oui, c'est _____.

2. Tu emmènes tes chaussures?

    Oui, _____.

3. J'emmène mon pantalon?

    Oui, _____.

4. Vous emmenez votre chien?

    Oui, _____.

5. C'est l'avion de Mounir, Fatiha et Thierry?

    Oui, _____.

6. Ils emmènent leurs lunettes?

    Oui, _____.

Possessive Adjectives

3

Check off the sentence that matches each picture.

1.
- ▨ a. Voilà ma brosse à dents.
- ▨ b. Voilà nos brosses à dents.
- ▨ c. Voilà ses brosses à dents.

2.
- ▨ a. C'est notre voiture.
- ▨ b. Ce sont leurs voitures.
- ▨ c. Ce sont vos voitures.

3.
- ▨ a. Vous emmenez mes lunettes de soleil?
- ▨ b. Vous emmenez vos lunettes de soleil?
- ▨ c. Vous emmenez vos chaussures?

4.
- ▨ a. Mounir emmène ses lunettes de soleil.
- ▨ b. Mounir emmène sa chaussure.
- ▨ c. Mounir emmène ses chaussures.

4

Connect the terms with their translations.

1. *his suitcase*	a. des valises
2. *your suitcase*	b. ta valise
3. *their suitcases*	c. leurs valises
4. *her suitcase*	d. nos valises
5. *our suitcases*	e. sa valise
6. *a hotel*	f. notre hôtel
7. *this hotel*	g. un hôtel
8. *our hotel*	h. cet hôtel
9. *your (pl.) hotel*	i. son hôtel
10. *her hotel*	j. votre hôtel

1

Julien is a new arrival at a newspaper office. He is welcomed by his colleagues. Matthieu introduces himself and his colleagues. Read the sentences and match up the pronouns with the appropriate sentences. You can also listen to the sentences on the CD.

1.  _____ m'appelle Mathieu.

2.  _____ s'appelle Raymond.

3.  Et _____ , c'est Marie.

4.  _____ sommes collègues.

> je – il – elle – nous – vous – ils – eux – tu

2

After everyone has introduced themselves to Julien, he naturally also wants to know what they all do and what their job is. Complete the sentences with the appropriate pronouns. You can also listen to the sentences on the CD.

1. _____ , c'est le directeur.

2. _____ , c'est Susan, elle fait un stage.

3. Et _____ , qu'est-ce que vous faites?

4. _____ , je fais les interviews.

5. _____ , Marie et Raymond, ils sont rédacteurs.

6. Et _____ , tu es le nouveau photographe!

> elle
> moi
> toi
> eux
> lui
> vous

5

Accentuating Personal Pronouns

3 ✎

Bon à savoir !

Subject pronoun forms:
je *(I)* – before a vowel or a mute **h**, shortened to **j'**
tu *(you)*
il – elle – on
(he, she, one)
nous *(we)*
vous *(you, plural or formal)*
ils – elles *(they)*
With persons of both sexes in the plural, **ils** is used.

Look at the pictures and complete the sentences with the appropriate pronouns.

1. _____ appelle une collègue.

2. _____ es gentil!

3. _____ téléphone.

4. _____ sommes joyeux!

5. _____ êtes Monsieur?

6. _____ sont journalistes.

4 ✎

In Julien's newspaper office there are a few coworkers who originally came from other parts of France. Read the first sentence and choose the correct pronoun from the second sentence.

1. Marie est Française. *Je / Elle / Elles* est de Rouen.
2. Yann est Français. *Je / Ils /Il* est de Grenoble.
3. Je suis Français. *Je / Il / Elle* suis de Perpignan.
4. Christine et Marc sont Français. *Nous / Ils / Il* sont de Paris.
5. Jeanne et Gaëlle sont Françaises. *Nous / Elles / Elle* sont de Lyon.
6. Je suis Français, et ma femme Mathilde aussi.
   Nous / Vous / Ils sommes de Perpignan.

5

In addition to the nonaccentuating personal pronouns, there are also accentuating pronouns. The forms are at the right in the **Bon à savoir** box.

The accentuating pronouns are used if they are "loose" in the sentence, that is, not placed directly before the verb, for example:

- to introduce someone
  Lui, c'est Raymond. *This is Raymond.*
- for emphasis, and in appositions
  Moi, je fais les interviews, et lui, il est rédacteur.
  I conduct the interviews and he is an editor.
- after the expressions **c'est** and **ce sont**
  Le chef, c'est vous! *You're the boss.*
- after prepositions and in combination with **et** or **ou**
  Je travaille avec eux au bureau. *I work with them at the office.*
  Lui et moi, nous sommes amis. *He and I are friends.*
- In sentences with no verb
  Qui prend du vin? Pas moi! *Who's having wine? Not me!*

Bon à savoir !

The forms of the accentuating personal pronoun:
moi
toi
lui – elle
nous
vous
eux – elles

6

Julien is trying to start up a band in his new company. He has already located two people and asks around to find out who plays which instruments. Look at some sentences from Julien's poll and write the appropriate accentuating personal pronouns in the spaces.

1. Nous cherchons des musiciens pour jouer avec _____ .

2. _____ , je joue du piano.

3. _____ , elle joue du violon.

4. _____ , il joue de la guitare et il chante.

5. Et _____ , tu aimes la musique?

6. Et _____ , vous jouez d'un instrument?

7 ✎

Marie, Susan, and Mounir want to go out tonight. The only question is *where*? They have the same preferences. A passerby, who overheard their conversation, gives them a tip.

Complete this conversation by writing the correct pronouns in the appropriate spaces.
You can also listen to the sentences on the CD.

Susan: _____ , Marie, _____ aimes le jazz.

Marie: Mounir, _____ , _____ aime le rap.

Susan: Et _____ , j'aime la techno.

Marie: Où allons-_____ ce soir, alors?

Un inconnu: _____ pouvez aller au café "Harmonie"?

Là-bas, ils jouent toutes les musiques!

> moi – lui – toi – il – tu- vous – nous

8 👓 🎧

Read the sentences and note how in the first sentence the name Julien, and in the second, the names Marie and Raymond, are replaced.

> **Mathieu présente Julien.** ▸ **Mathieu le présente.**
> **Mathieu présente Marie et Raymond.** ▸ **Mathieu les présente.**

Direct object pronouns designate things and persons in the sentence that do not perform actions, but rather are acted upon. In the sentence they answer the question *whom?* **or** *what?*

> **Je mange la pomme** ▸ **Je la mange.**

The forms of the direct object pronouns are at the right in the **Bon à savoir** box.

Note the forms of the third person: Don't confuse the forms **le – la – l' – les** with the articles **le – la – l' – les**. These forms can stand for either people or things:

> **Je regarde Marie.** ▸ **Je la regarde.**
> **Je regarde la photo.** ▸ **Je la regarde.**

In the sentence they are placed
- before the verb, including in negative sentences:
  Je mange les gâteaux. – Je ne les mange pas.
- before an infinitive that follows a verb in the sentence:
  Je voudrais bien les manger.

9 ✏️

The direct object pronouns are missing from these sentences. Write the appropriate pronouns in the blanks by replacing the words in bold type.

1. J'ai des **lettres**. Je _____ poste.

2. Où est mon **manteau**? Tiens, _____ voilà!

3. J'aime bien cette **photo**, je _____ regarde souvent.

4. J'aime bien ces **chaussures**, je _____ achète.

5. **Tu** me donnes ton numéro de téléphone? Je _____ appelle ce soir.

10 👓

Read the sentences and note how in the first sentence the name Mathieu, and in the second, the names Mathieu and Marie, are replaced.

Julien donne la main à Mathieu. ▸ Julien lui donne la main.
Julien donne la main à Mathieu et Marie. ▸
Julien leur donne la main.

The indirect object pronouns refer to the people in the sentence who do not perform the action, but function as objects. In the sentence they correspond to the question *to whom?, for whom?, to what,* and *for what?,* and they replace objects of the preposition **à**.

Je donne la lettre à Susan. ▸ Je lui donne la lettre.

The forms of the indirect object pronouns are at the left in the **Bon à savoir** box.

Unlike the direct object pronouns, **lui** and **leur** refer only to people. For other prepositional groups with **à**, the pronoun **y** is used:

Je pense au week-end. ▸ J'y pense.

The indirect object pronouns are placed:
* before the verb, including in negative sentences:
Je lui parle. Je ne leur parle pas.
* before the infinitive that follows a verb in a sentence.
J'aime leur parler.

11 ✏

Mathieu is telling about himself and his girlfriend in Rouen. Fill in the blanks with the correct direct or indirect object pronouns.

1. J'habite à Paris et ma copine Sophie à Rouen, mais je _____ téléphone souvent.

2. C'est cher, mais je _____ appelle quand même tous les soirs!

3. Sophie a un petit frère, je _____ trouve drôle.

4. Il fait toujours des bêtises, mais toute la famille _____ aime bien.

5. Je _____ donne souvent des gâteaux, alors il m'adore!

6. Les parents de Sophie, je _____ trouve aussi super sympas.

   Ils _____ invitent souvent.

7. Je _____ amène souvent du vin, ils adorent ça! Toute la famille _____ aime bien!

12 ✏️ 👓

The pronoun **y** replaces constructions with **à** inside a sentence; the pronoun **en** replaces constructions with **de**.

Write the appropriate pronouns (**y** or **en**) in the blanks:

1. Il parle de son travail. Il _____ parle.

2. Je pense au week-end. J'_____ pense.

3. Vous achetez des bananes? Oui, nous _____ achetons.

4. Tu es au bureau? Oui, j'_____ suis.

In a sentence **y** is used in place of:
- prepositional groups containing a verb + **à**
  Je pense au week-end. J'y pense.
- designations of place with **à**, **dans**, **sur**, **chez**, or other prepositions
  Tu restes au bureau ce soir? Oui, j'y reste.
  Tu es chez toi? Oui, j'y suis.

En is used in place of
- prepositional groups with a verb + **de**
  Il parle de son travail. Il en parle.
- constructions with an indefinite article, a partitive article, or a specification of quantity
  Tu as une voiture? Oui, j'en ai une, Pierre en a deux.
  Tu prends du sucre? Oui, j'en prends.
  Tu as un peu de farine pour faire des crêpes? Oui, il en faut seulement 100 grammes.
- designations of place with **de**
  Tu viens de la gare? Oui, j'en viens.

13 ✏️

Write the sentences using an adverbial pronoun in the blanks. Replace the phrases in bold print with the pronouns **y** or **en**.

1. Marc et Marion sont **au bureau**. _____

2. Demain, je reste **à la maison**. _____

3. Nous mangeons **de la tarte aux pommes**. _____

4. Il pense toujours **à son travail**. _____

5. J'ai besoin **de nouvelles chaussures**. _____

6. Il y a encore **des places**. _____

14 🖉

These sentences are all scrambled up. Put the words back into the right sequence.

1. la / Nous / trouvons / jolie / . _____

2. moi / avec / Il / la télé / regarde / . _____

3. téléphonent / te / Ils / souvent / . _____

4. lui / il / donne / la main. _____

5. parle / Elle / lui / à / . _____

6. à / Vous / eux / pensez / . _____

7. Je / voudrais / en / manger / . _____

8. Tu / à la maison/ restes? / J' / reste / y / Oui, _____

15 🖉

Julien wants to celebrate his new job in the company and decides to make a **mousse au chocolat** for his colleagues. His wife Mathilde will help him, but he has to do the shopping by himself. Mathilde asks what's already on hand and what must be bought. Complete Julien's answers according to the pattern:

Tu manges la mousse au chocolat? Oui, je la mange.

1. Tes collègues, ils aiment la mousse au chocolat?

   Bien sûr, ils _____ aiment.

2. Alors, tu as le chocolat?

   Oui, je _____ ai.

3. Tu achètes aussi le beurre?

   Oui, je _____ achète demain.

4. Et tu penses à acheter les œufs?

   Oui, j'_____ pense.

5. Et le sel? Nous avons du sel?

   Mais oui, Mathilde, nous _____ avons encore

1 🖉

Write the missing pronouns in the blanks.

1. Marc et moi, _____ mangeons au restaurant.

2. Marc et _____ , vous avez de la chance.

3. Moi, cet après-midi, _____ reste au bureau.

4. Mais ce soir, je regarde un film à la télé, vous le regardez avec _____ ?

5. Mes cousins m'invitent souvent à manger chez _____ .

6. Mais Marc, _____ , il n'a jamais le temps le soir.

7. Et Marie? Tu penses qu'_____ a le temps?

2 🖉

Answer these questions with **Oui, . . .** and construct the answer according to this pattern: **Marie achète les chaussures? Oui, Marie les achète.**

1. Marie est là?   _____

2. Il appelle Marie?   _____

3. On téléphone à Marie?   _____

4. Est-ce que Thierry et Fatiha sont là? _____

5. Est-ce qu'il appelle Thierry et Fatiha? _____

6. On téléphone à Thierry et Fatiha?   _____

3 TR.26 🖉

Read the sentences and underline the correct pronouns in the second part of each sentence. You can listen to the sentences again if you wish.

1. Nous habitons à Marseille. Nous y / — / en habitons.
2. Elle travaille en Angleterre. Elle y / — / en travaille.
3. Nous achetons du lait. Nous y / — / en achetons.
4. Je voudrais un paquet de thé. J'y / — / en voudrais.
5. Il y a trop de voitures. Il y y / — / en a trop.
6. Nous pensons à acheter du lait. Nous y / — / en pensons.

4

Choose the correct answer to the question, or the correct expression, and check the appropriate box.

1. Marie et Susan sont à Paris?

   ☐ a. Oui, elle y est.
   ☐ b. Oui, ils y sont.
   ☐ c. Oui, elles y sont.

2. On appelle Thierry et Mounir?

   ☐ a. Oui, on l'appelle.
   ☐ b. Oui, on les appelle.
   ☐ c. Oui, ils les appellent.

3. Tu manges ta pomme?

   ☐ a. Oui, je le mange.
   ☐ b. Oui, je la mange.
   ☐ c. Oui, je les mange.

4. Il reste du chocolat?

   ☐ a. Oui, il en reste.
   ☐ b. Oui, il y reste.
   ☐ c. Non, je n'y reste pas.

5. Tu restes au bureau ce soir?

   ☐ a. Non, je n'y reste pas.
   ☐ b. Oui, il en reste.
   ☐ c. Oui, nous y restons.

6. Raymond parle toujours de son travail.

   ☐ a. Il lui parle toujours.
   ☐ b. Il en parle toujours.
   ☐ c. Il parle toujours de lui.

7. Je pense souvent à Caroline et Pierre.

   ☐ a. J'y pense souvent.
   ☐ b. Je pense souvent à eux.
   ☐ c. Ils pensent souvent à eux.

8. Nous parlons de notre nouveau chef.

   ☐ a. Nous en parlons.
   ☐ b. Nous parlons de lui.
   ☐ c. Nous lui parlons.

9. Il parle de sa voiture.

   ☐ a. Il parle d'elle.
   ☐ b. Il en parle.
   ☐ c. Il lui parle.

1

Look at the picture of Mrs. Duval's wedding and read the sentences that describe the photo. Pay attention to the adjectives and their various forms.

1. Mme Duval a des roses rouges dans les mains.
2. La dame à gauche porte une robe rouge et un chapeau rouge.
3. La dame à côté de Mme Duval porte un chapeau vert et des chaussures vertes.
4. La voiture des mariés est verte.
5. Les mariés sont devant une petite église.
6. A gauche, on voit un petit chien.
7. A droite, des petits enfants ont des petites fleurs.

2 [TR. 27]

Madame Duval shows her wedding photo (see above) to her granddaughter Marie. Read her descriptions and match them up with the correct shortened descriptions. You can also listen to Mme Duval's statements on the CD.

1. Regarde, Marie comme nous sommes jeunes sur la photo, Jean et moi!
2. Moi, je suis petite.
3. Lui, il est grand.
4. Sa sœur, Julie, est très grande!
5. Regarde, son mari, Pierre, il est vraiment petit.
6. Et mon père, il est vraiment heureux!
7. Ma mère est heureuse aussi.
8. Mais Mme Moulin est très triste!
9. Sa robe est rouge comme son nez, mais quelle couleur pour une robe!

a. Il est grand.	b. Elle est grande.	c. Je suis petite.
d. Il est petit.	e. Elle est triste.	f. Nous sommes jeunes.
g. Il est heureux.	h. Elle est heureuse.	i. Son nez est rouge.

3

Adjectives are used to describe and identify things or people, and often refer to a noun, a subject pronoun, or a proper name; they agree in number and gender with the noun or person they describe.

- masculine / feminine: masculine form + **-e** ▶ feminine form
  grand, grande – bleu, bleue
  If the masculine form ends in **-e**, the feminine is the same:
  rouge, rouge.
  In the **Bon à savoir** box you will find adjectives that exhibit peculiarities in the formation of their feminine form.
- Singular / Plural: Singular + **-s** (silent).
  intelligent, intelligents – grand, grands
  If the masculine singular form already ends in **-s** or **-x**, the plural form doesn't change: **heureux, heureux**

Fill in the blanks with the correct endings.

1. Il est grand. Elle est grand_____. Ils sont grand_____

2. Il est blond. Elle est blond_____. Ils sont blond_____.

3. Je suis heureux. Elle est heureu_____. Ils sont heureu_____.

4

The adjectives **beau**, **nouveau**, and **vieux** refer to noteworthy features.
Singular forms: before consonants: **beau, nouveau, vieux.**
Before vowels or a mute **h: bel, nouvel, vieil.**
Masculine plural forms: **beaux, nouveaux, vieux.**
Feminine plural forms: **belles, nouvelles, vieilles.**

Marie and her grandmother will show you some useful sentences for saying where someone lives. Write the correct forms of the adjectives in the blanks.

1. J'habite dans un _____ quartier, j'ai un _____ appartement dans une _____ maison. (vieux, vieille, vieil)

2. Moi, j'habite dans un _____ quartier, j'ai un _____ apparte-ment dans une _____ maison. (nouvel, nouvelle, nouveau)

3. En fait, j'habite dans un _____ quartier, j'ai un _____ appartement dans une très _____ maison! (beau, belle, bel)

5

Which adjectives are masculine, and which are feminine? Write them in the correct column in the chart.

masculine	feminine

a. vieille – b. gros –
c. heureuse – d. belle –
e. gentille – f. longue –
g. nouvel – h. bel –
i. blanc – j. conservatrice –
k. publique

6 [TR. 28]

Madame Duval is in the shoe store in which Mounir, a friend of her grand-daughter Marie, works. Read the dialogue and mark off all the adjectives that come directly before a noun. You can listen to the dialogue on the CD.

Mounir: Bonjour Madame, je peux vous aider?

Mme Duval: Bonjour! Je voudrais acheter de nouvelles chaussures…

Mounir: Vous avez une idée précise?

Mme Duval: Ah, je voudrais de belles chaussures… et surtout confortables!

Mounir: Oui, c'est important! Qu'est-ce que vous pensez de cette paire rouge et blanche?

Mme Duval: Hmm… je préfère les couleurs discrètes! Ces chaussures noires, elles sont jolies… Mais elles sont trop grandes, j'ai de petits pieds, moi! Je fais du 36 ou du 37.

Mounir: Bon, je vais chercher les deux tailles.

Mounir: Voilà, Madame!

Mme Duval: Merci, jeune homme… Mais maintenant je voudrais ces chaussures jaunes!

Mounir: Mais… le jaune, ce n'est pas très discret, Madame!

Mme Duval: Ce n'est pas grave! C'est l'été! Combien est-ce qu'elles coûtent?

Mounir: 59 Euros…

Mme Duval: Oh là là… La vie est chère, aujourd'hui!

Mounir: Mais pour deux paires de chaussures, on fait une petite réduction! 70 Euros pour les deux paires, la noire et la jaune!

Mme Duval: Oh, vous êtes gentil! C'est un bon prix. Je suis très contente!

Adjectives of Color

7 ✏

There are many types of shoes. Write the appropriate translations for the sentences below. The adjectives of color are in the box.

1. black shoes

_____

2. red shoes

_____

3. orange shoes

_____

4. green shoes

_____

noir – *black*	**bleu** – *blue*	**blanc** – *white*	**marron** – *brown*
rouge – *red*	**orange** – *orange*	**vert** – *green*	

8 ✏

Adjective placement in French:
- usually after the noun
  une couleur discrète – des chaussures noires
- short, commonly used adjectives (**grand**, **gros**, **petit**, **jeune**, **vieux**, **bon**, **mauvais**, **beau**, **joli**, **nouveau**): before the noun
  une petite maison – un beau jardin
- connected to a noun by a verb: in this case, too, the adjective must agree with the noun:
  Marie est gentille.

Write the correct adjective in the appropriate blank.

1. Vous avez une idée _____ ?

2. Ces chaussures _____ , elles sont jolies ...

3. Bonjour, je voudrais acheter de _____ chaussures.

4. C'est un _____ prix.

a. noires – b. nouvelles – c. bon – d. précise

9 🖉

These sentences are scrambled. Put the words back in the right order.

1. cherche / nouvelles / Madame Duval / chaussures / de.

_____

2. chaussures / et / rouges / blanches / des / Il y a.

_____

3. préfère / Madame Duval / petites / les / noires / chaussures.

_____

4. sont / Elles / discrètes / élégantes / et.

_____

5. jaune / aussi / Il y a / jolie / une / paire.

_____

10 TR.29 👓

The adjectives of number are used to specify the number of persons and things.

The cardinal numbers from 0–20: Read the lines that Fatiha has dictated and pay attention to the numbers:
Un, deux, trois, Fatiha c'est moi! (1, 2, 3)
Quatre, cinq, six, Thierry aime le pastis. (4, 5, 6)
Sept, huit, neuf et dix, moi, je préfère le cassis. (7, 8, 9, 10)

Thierry has continued with the numbers from 11 through 20:
Onze, douze, treize, Mounir mange des merguez. (11, 12, 13)
Quatorze, quinze, seize, c'est une spécialité française. (14, 15, 16)
Dix-sept, dix-huit, dix-neuf et vingt – mais non! C'est marocain!
(17, 18, 19, 20)

Cardinal numbers from 20–99, 100, and 1000:
Look at the designations for the tens and read them aloud:
20 **vingt**, 30 **trente**, 40 **quarante**, 50 **cinquante**
60 **soixante**, 70 **soixante-dix**, 80 **quatre-vingts**, 90 **quatre-vingt-dix**
100 **cent**, 1000 **mille**

You can also listen to the poem as well as the individual numbers on the CD.

Bon à savoir !

The number **un**, **une** agrees in gender with the noun; this applies to all numbers involving **un**, **une**:
un tee-shirt, une robe, vingt-et-une disquettes

The numbers from 70 through 79 and from 90 to 99 are not constructed with the numbers from 1 through 9, but rather with the numbers following 10:
70 **soixante-dix**,
71 **soixante et onze**,
72 **soixante-douze**...
91 **quatre-vingt-onze**,
94 **quatre-vingt-quatorze**,
99 **quatre-vingt-dix-neuf**...

The word **et** is used in 21, 31, 41, 51, 61, and 71:
21 **vingt et un**
41 **quarante et un**
But **et** is not used in 81, 101, and 1001:
81 **quatre-vingt-un**
101 **cent un**
1001 **mille un**

6

Ordinal Numbers

11 ✎

Look at the illustration: which runner finishes in which place? Match the numbers of the runners with the ordinal numbers.

1. _____ ,

c'est le numéro 6.

2. _____ ,

c'est le numéro 2.

3. _____ ,

c'est le numéro 41.

a. le deuxième – b. le premier – c. le troisième

Ordinal numbers are used for enumerating individual parts of a series. They are constructed by adding the ending **-ième** to the appropriate cardinal number and putting the definite article before the counting word:
le – la sixième, **le – la quarante-huitième**, **le – la centième**
Special cases: **le – la quatrième**, **le – la cinquième**, **le – la neuvième**

12 ✎

Have you ever been to Paris? Because the city is so large, it is divided into precincts, the **arrondissements**. Look at the map of Paris and cross out the statements that are not true.

1. Paris a trente arrondissements.
2. Le premier arrondissement est au centre.
3. La Tour Eiffel est dans le treizième arrondissement.
4. Notre-Dame est dans le cinquième arrondissement.
5. La Seine passe dans le dix-septième arrondissement.
6. Le Louvre est dans le onzième arrondissement.

Les 20 arrondissments de Paris:

Bon à savoir !

The cardinal numbers are used in specifying dates:
le 14 juillet
le 31 décembre
The ordinal number is used only with the first day of the month:
le 1er janvier.

Bon à savoir !

Some more special considerations:
– Before both ordinal and cardinal numbers no apostrophe is used:
le – la huitième,
le – la onzième
– For the number 1 there is a masculine and a feminine form: **le premier – la première.**
However, they cannot be joined to other numbers; thus, **le – la vingt-et-unième**
– The ordinal numbers are written in a short form with an **-e**:
2e, **45e**..., a special form is **1er**, **1ère**

13

Marie is curious to know if her grandmother has bought new shoes or not, and she needs the phone number of a **chocolatier**. Read the phone conversation and choose the correct adjective in each case.

1. Allo Mamie? Alors, tu as de *nouvel / nouvelles / nouvelle* chaussures maintenant?
2. Oui, j'ai deux paires, une paire *noir / noires / noire* et une paire jaune…
3. Et c'est une *bon / bonne / bonnes* affaire! Merci de tes *bon / bons / bonne* conseils!
4. Je suis *content / contente / contents* pour toi! Moi aussi, il me faut un *petit / petite / petits* conseil…
5. … je voudrais acheter des chocolats, est-ce qu'il y a une *bon / bonne / bonnes* chocolaterie dans ton quartier?
6. Oui, il y en a une très bonne mais un peu *cher / chère / chers* boulevard Lacroix!
7. Tu as leur adresse *précis / précise / précises*?
   Euh, oui, c'est 42, boulevard Lacroix. Et leur numéro de téléphone, c'est le 01-43-82-11-14.

14

Marie has two American friends; she tells her grandmother about them. Write the correct adjectives in the blanks. Pay attention to the correct forms and their placement.

1. Tanya et Julia sont _____ filles _____. (deux – américain)
2. Elles sont de _____ amies. (vieux)
3. Tanya est _____, elle a de _____ yeux _____.
   (blond, bleu, grand)
4. Son copain s'appelle Jean-Pierre, il est _____. (Français)
5. C'est un _____ homme… et il est si _____! (beau, gentil)
6. Julia, elle, est _____ et _____ et elle aussi a un copain en France. (petit, blond)
7. Il est aussi très _____. Pour lui rendre visite, elle fait de _____ voyages. (sympa, long)
8. Elle aime beaucoup les _____ vacances! (grand)

Bon à savoir !

In France the phone numbers have ten digits:
– the first two provide information about the region: 01 = Paris and the surrounding area;
– the following numbers are then said in groups of two;
– 01 40 80 71 23 is thus "**zéro un, quarante, quatre-vingts, soixante et onze, vingt-trois.**"

15

Here are a number of expressions and titles with adjectives. Match them up with their correct translations.

1. Jamais deux sans trois.	a. *Little Red Riding Hood*
2. les grandes vacances	b. *the Yellow Pages*
3. le petit chaperon rouge	c. *the roller coaster*
4. le quatorze juillet	d. *All good things come in threes.*
5. la Maison Blanche	e. *July 14 / the Revolution*
6. le septième ciel	f. *Summer vacation*
7. les Verts	g. *The White House*
8. le premier janvier	h. *Seventh heaven*
9. les Pages jaunes	i. *New Year*
10. le grand huit	j. *The Greens, Green Party*

16

Write the number under each picture.

1. _____

2. _____

3. _____

4. _____

1

Use the same adjective, but be sure to write it in the correct form and make it agree with the noun:

1. un homme pauvre, des femmes _____

2. le premier janvier, la _____ année

3. une femme rêveuse, un enfant _____

4. des gros messieurs, une _____ valise

5. un long pull, une _____ robe

6. des grandes maisons, un _____ appartement

7. un nouveau vélo, des _____ voitures

2

Read the statements and decide which picture they correspond to.

1. Il est vert.

☐ a. ☐ b. ☐ c.

2. les Pages jaunes

☐ a. ☐ b. ☐ c.

3. Il y a trois livres rouges.

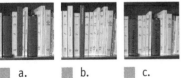

☐ a. ☐ b. ☐ c.

4. Les Dupont habitent au soixante-et-onze.

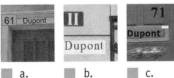

☐ a. ☐ b. ☐ c.

5. Je vais au quatrième.

☐ a. ☐ b. ☐ c.

Adjectives / Numbers

3 🖊

In the following sentences one thing is negated and another is implied. Write the opposite adjectives in the appropriate forms.

1. Cette voiture n'est pas nouvelle, elle est _____.

2. Mon professeur n'est pas vieux, il est _____.

3. Ce film n'est pas bon, il est _____.

4. Ces lunettes de soleil ne sont pas bon marché, elles sont _____.

5. Les enfants de Julien ne sont pas petits, ils sont _____.

4 🖊

Here are some numbers that are not written out and some numbers that are written out but not given in numerical form. Fill in the blanks.

Example: **5 ▶ cinq   vingt-trois ▶ 23**

a. 18 ▶ _____	k. vingt-huit	▶ _____
b. 36 ▶ _____	l. quatre-vingt-quinze ▶ _____
c. 14 ▶ _____	m. treize	▶ _____
d. 6 ▶ _____	n. dix	▶ _____
e. 78 ▶ _____	o. quarante-sept	▶ _____
f. 55 ▶ _____	p. soixante-douze	▶ _____
g. 11 ▶ _____	q. cent	▶ _____
h. 0 ▶ _____	r. deux	▶ _____
i. 68 ▶ _____	s. seize	▶ _____
j. 80 ▶ _____	t. trente-neuf	▶ _____

Aller and other Verbs

1

Marie brings Mounir to the airport. By chance they meet Susan in the parking lot. Read the conversation between Mounir, Marie, and Susan, and check off all the forms of the verb **aller**. You can also listen to the dialogue on the CD.

Susan: Salut vous deux, vous allez bien?
Mounir + Marie: Oui, nous allons bien, et toi?
Susan: Ça va!

Susan: Tu pars en vacances, Mounir?
Mounir: Oui, je vais en vacances avec mon oncle et ma tante.
Susan: Et vous allez où?
Marie: Ils vont à Marseille!

2

There are many irregular French verbs. Look at the various conjugations and let them sink in. Many forms sound alike.

1. **dormir** –
   je dors, tu dors, il dort, nous dormons, vous dormez, ils dorment
2. **sortir** –
   je sors, tu sors, il sort, nous sortons, vous sortez, ils sortent
3. **vouloir** –
   je veux, tu veux, il veut, nous voulons, vous voulez, ils veulent
4. **devoir** –
   je dois, tu dois, il doit, nous devons, vous devez, ils doivent
5. **aller** –
   je vais, tu vas, il va, nous allons, vous allez, ils vont

Aller + *venir* / *Verbs of the 3rd group ending in* **-ir**

3

Put the forms of the verb **aller** in the right order:

1. tu vas – je vais – il va _____

2. ils vont – vous allez – nous allons _____

aller	
je vais	nous allons
tu vas	vous allez
il va	ils vont

venir	
je viens	nous venons
tu viens	vous venez
il vient	ils viennent

devenir	
je deviens	
tu deviens	
il devient	
nous devenons	
vous devenez	
ils viennent	

The verb **aller** has several meanings; it can be used to express
- where someone is going: **aller** + location
  Vous allez où? Nous allons à Marseille.
- how someone is going: **aller** + means of transportation
  Vous allez à pied? Mais non, nous allons en voiture.
- how someone feels: **aller bien / mal**
  Comment allez vous? Je vais bien, merci!

The verbs **venir** and **devenir** are irregular. Look at these examples:

> **Et toi, Susan, tu viens d'où? Je viens de Londres.**
> **Et lui, il vient de San Francisco.**
> **Vous venez, l'avion part bientôt! Oui, nous venons.**
> **Thierry et Fatiha viennent avec leurs valises.**

The conjugations of **aller** and **venir** are in the conjugation boxes at the left.

4

In contrast to **-ir** verbs in the second group, third-group verbs ending in **-ir** don't use **-ss** in the plural. So in this case the endings are **-s**, **-s**, **-t**, **-ons**, **-ez**, **-ent**. If the verb has two consonants in the stem before the ending, the second one is eliminated in the singular; otherwise there would be three consonants in a row: **dormir – je dors**, **tu dors**, **il dort**.

But the plural ending begins with a vowel, so the consonant is retained: **nous dormons**, **vous dormez**, **ils dorment**.

partir	
je pars	nous partons
tu pars	vous partez
il part	ils partent

Bon à savoir !

The following verbs are conjugated in the same way:
sortir – *to go out*
sentir – *to feel, smell*
dormir – *to sleep*
servir – *to serve*
courir – *to run*

Now apply these rules to the verb **partir** and fill in the blanks. You will find the conjugation of **partir** in the conjugation box.

je _____ nous _____

tu _____ vous _____

il _____ ils _____

> Et toi, Marie, tu pars aussi ?
> Je pars en vacances !
> Non, nous ne partons pas ensemble.

part – pars – partez – partons – pars – partent

5 ✎

All these photos correspond to descriptions using verbs of the 3rd group ending in **-ir**. Write the sentences under the corresponding photos.

1. _____ 2. _____ 3. _____ 4. _____

5. _____ 6. _____ 7. _____ 8. _____

> a. Ça sent bon! – b. Ils courent. – c. Nous partons en voyage. –
> d. Elle ouvre la porte. – e. Il dort! – f. Ils dorment. –
> g. Je vous sers un apéritif? – h. Je sors.

6 ✎

Look at the conjugation of the verb **voir**. Which forms resemble one another?

je vois, tu vois, il voit, nous voyons, vous voyez, ils voient

Now try to plug in the missing forms. A little hint: The first two forms in the singular always sound the same; the first two forms in the plural always display the same peculiarity, and the third person in the plural resembles the first and second.

1. j'attends – tu _____ – il attend – nous attendons –

   vous _____ – ils attendent

2. je crois – tu crois – il _____ – nous croyons – vous croyez –

   ils _____

3. je _____ – tu bois – il boit – nous _____ –

   vous buvez – ils boivent

4. je mets – tu _____ – il met – nous mettons –

   vous _____ – ils mettent

Bon à savoir !

When a **-d** crops up before an ending in **-re**, as in **attendre**, the last letter of the third person singular is not **-t**, but rather **-d: il attend**. The same applies to **rendre, entendre, perdre, vendre.**

Special forms:
prendre, apprendre:
nous prenons, vous prenez, ils prennent

mettre:
je mets, tu mets, il met

conduire, lire:
nous conduisons, vous conduisez, ils conduisent
nou lisons, vous lisez, ils lisent

voir, revoir, croire:
nous voyons, vous voyez
nous croyons, vous croyez

boire:
nous buvons, vous buvez, ils boivent

connaître, disparaître, naître:
nous connaissons, vous connaissez, ils connaissent
nous disparaissons...
nous naissons...

---

attendez – bois –
croient – attends –
croit – buvons –
mets – mettez

Dire and *faire*

7

Look at the pictures and read what the various people say. Pay special attention to the verb forms.

faire	
je fais	nous faisons
tu fais	vous faites
il fait	ils font

Non !

Peut–être!

1. Qu'est-ce que vous en dites?
2. Je dis oui.
3. Il dit non.
4. Nous disons: peut-être!

dire	
je dis	nous disons
tu dis	vous dites
il dit	ils ditent

5. Ils ne disent rien.
6. Je fais du sport.
7. Tu fais de la natation.
8. Elle fait la cuisine.

Bon à savoir !

There's a lot you can do with **faire**. There are several meanings:
– *to make, to do* in the usual sense
  Faites comme chez vous!
  Ils font du bruit.
– **faire** + the designation of an action
  faire le ménage
  faire ses devoirs
  faire la cuisine
  faire la vaisselle
  faire un gâteau
– for leisure time activities
  faire du sport, faire du tennis, faire du cheval *(to go horseback riding)*

9. Vous faites de la musique.
10. Ils ne font rien!

8 ✏

The parents and brothers and sisters are expecting Marie and her grand-mother today. Everything is in a state of agitation . . . and the things that still need to be done in the house are divided up. Write the appropriate forms of the verb **faire** in the blanks.

1. Je _____ le ménage dans le salon.

2. Papa et moi, nous _____ la cuisine.

3. Thomas et Sophie _____ la vaisselle.

4. Allez, les enfants, _____ vite!

5. Oui, oui, on _____ ce qu'on peut!

9

Look at the examples in the illustrations using the verbs **pouvoir**, **vouloir**, and **devoir**. These are modal verbs that are used in conjunction with other verbs in the infinitive. You will find their forms at the right.

vouloir	manger
pouvoir	manger
devoir	manger

vouloir	je veux	nous voulons
	tu veux	vous voulez
	il veut	ils veulent
pouvoir	je peux	nous pouvons
	tu peux	vous pouvez
	il peut	ils peuvent
devoir	je dois	nous devons
	tu dois	vous devez
	il doit	ils doivent

savoir	
je sais	nous savons
tu sais	vous savez
il sait	ils savent

Another modal verb is **falloir**; however, it is used only in the third person singular as the impersonal expression **il faut**.

Il faut choisir vite. *You have to choose quickly.*
Il faut de la farine pour faire des crêpes.
You need flour to make crêpes.
Il faut apprendre beaucoup dans cette leçon!
There's a lot we have to learn in this lesson.

10 ✏️

Marie and her grandmother have arrived at the parents' house in Normandy. Now they are eating at the table. Then someone asks who wants wine to drink . . . and who may have it.
Complete the dialogue with the correct verb forms.

1. **Mme Duval:** Vous _____ du vin?

2. **Mamie:** Bien sûr que nous _____ du vin!

3. **Marie:** Moi, un tout petit peu ... Je _____ conduire!

4. **M. Duval:** Ah, boire ou conduire, il _____ choisir!

5. **Thomas:** Moi, je _____ bien du vin.

6. **Mme Duval:** Toi, Thomas, tu as 12 ans, tu ne _____ pas boire

d'alcool!

veux
voulons
voulez
peux
dois
faut

11 ✏️

Forms of **savoir** and **pouvoir** are missing from these sentences. The **Bon à savoir** box contains some tips on usage.

1. Où est le maillot de bain? Sans maillot de bain, Mounir ne _____ pas nager!

2. Il y a un restaurant tout près d'ici, nous _____ manger là-bas!

3. Est-ce que je _____ vous aider?

4. Il a mal à la tête, il ne _____ pas rester longtemps au soleil.

5. Ce Mathieu, c'est un vrai play-boy. Il _____ parler aux femmes!

6. J'ai seulement 16 ans, je ne _____ pas boire d'alcool.

7. Je _____ conduire, mais ici je ne _____ pas, nous n'avons pas de voiture!

8. Tous les Marocains _____ parler français.

12 👓

With reflexive verbs the action reflects back on the person performing the action. Look at the following examples:
* nonreflexive: **Il lave la vaisselle.** *He washes the dishes.*
* reflexive: **Il se lave.** *He washes (himself).*

The verb forms remain the same, whether or not they are reflexive. All you have to watch out for are the reflexive pronouns:
me, **te**, **se**, **nous**, **vous**, **se**. **Me**, **te**, and **se** contract before a vowel or a mute **h: je m'amuse**. All the forms of **se laver** are in the conjugation box.

se laver

je me lave
tu te laves
il se lave

nous nous lavons
vous vous lavez
ils se lavent

Here are several reflexive verbs:
* regular **-er** verbs: **se coucher** – *to go to bed*; **se laver** – *to wash*; **se marier** – *to get married*; **se promener** – *to take a walk*
* regular **-er** verbs with some special cases: **se changer** – *to change clothes*; **se lever** – *to get up, stand up*
* 3rd group **-ir** verbs: **s'endormir** – *to fall asleep*; **se sentir** – *to feel*; **se connaître** – *to know oneself, one another*

Most French reflexive verbs are not reflexive in English, for example, **se lever, se coucher, s'endormir, se promener, se marier**.
Reflexive verbs are more common in French than in English. Examples of English reflexive verbs are *to deceive oneself* and *to flatter oneself*.

13 ✎

The reflexive pronouns are missing from the following sentences. Write them in the appropriate spaces.

1. Demain, nous _____ levons à six heures.

2. Je ne _____ sens pas bien.

3. Vous pouvez _____ laver les mains dans la cuisine.

4. Elle va _____ promener à Montmartre.

5. Thomas, tu _____ lèves? Il est 10 heures…

6. Ils _____ connaissent depuis vingt ans et ils

   _____ aiment comme au premier jour.

14 ✎

Marie is originally from Normandy, but because of her work she moved to Paris, where her grandmother lives. Now it's summer vacation and she is traveling with her to visit her parents. Complete the dialogue with Susan, using the appropriate forms of the verbs **aller**, **venir**, **dormir**, and **partir**. You can also listen to the dialogue on the CD.

1. **Susan:** Et toi, tu *pars / pas / part* aussi en vacances?

2. **Marie:** Oui et non, je *vais / vas / va* chez mes parents.

3. **Marie:** Ma grand-mère *vient / viens / viennent* aussi. Mais la maison est

   très petite, nous *dors / dormons / dorment* tous dans une seule chambre!

4. **Susan:** Pourquoi tu ne *viens / vient / viennent* pas en Angleterre avec

   moi? Julien et sa famille *viens / vient / viennent* aussi.

5. **Marie:** Vous *partent / part / partez* quand?

6. **Susan:** Nous *partons / part / partent* déjà demain…

   le train *partons / part / partent* à 6 heures du matin.

7. **Marie:** C'est dommage, mais je *vais / vas / va* chez mes parents déjà ce

   week-end. Ils habitent en Normandie.

8. **Susan:** Alors tu *pars / part / partent* en Normandie! Quelle chance

   d'avoir des parents là-bas!

15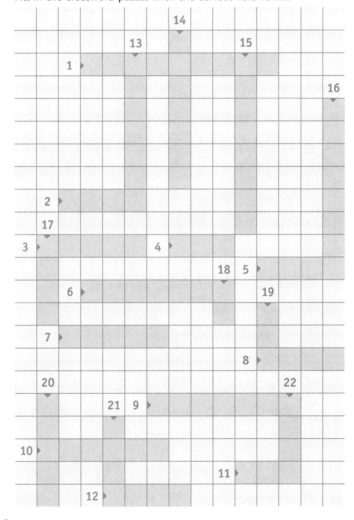

One verb form that comes from a different source than the other ones has slipped in. Cross it out.

1. tu viens – il vient – nous venons – ils vont
2. je veux – il voit – nous voulons – ils veulent
3. je vais – elle veut – il va – vous allez
4. je dors – tu dors – il doit – nous dormons
5. tu dois – il doit – nous devons – ils disent

16

Fill in the crossword puzzle with the correct verb forms.

Horizontal
1. promettre, vous…
2. faire, ils…
3. dire, vous…
4. aller, tu…
5. voir, il…
6. vouloir, ils…
7. prendre, il…
8. sentir, il…
9. connaître, je…
10. savoir, nous…
11. rire, il…
12. sortir, je…

Vertical
13. offrir, ils…
14. pouvoir, ils…
15. entendre, vous…
16. venir, ils…
17. devoir, tu…
18. se lever, tu…lèves
19. dire, tu…
20. lire, vous…
21. boire, tu…
22. savoir, il…

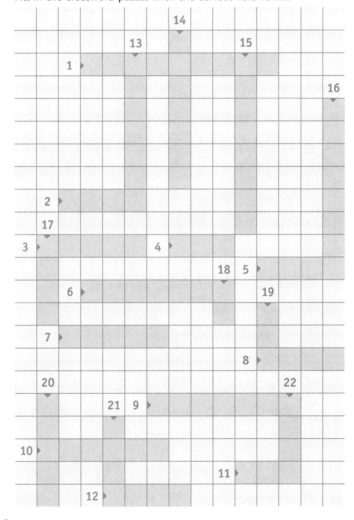

1 ✎

Look at the illustrations and write the correct descriptions below them.

1. _____ 2. _____ 3. _____ 4. _____

5. _____ 6. _____ 7. _____ 8. _____

a. il dort – b. il se lève – c. ils boivent – d. elle lit –
e. il fait beau – f. ils s'amusent – g. il se promène – h. il boit

2 ✎

Connect the terms with their translations.

1. *they come*	a. ils vont
2. *they go*	b. j'apprends
3. *I wait*	c. nous croyons
4. *I learn*	d. vous dites
5. *we understand*	e. nous connaissons
6. *we believe*	f. nous comprenons
7. *we know*	g. ils viennent
8. *you say*	h. vous voulez
9. *you should*	i. vous devez
10. *you want*	j. j'attends

Verbs

3 🖉

Break apart the strings of letters into individual words.

1. nousdevonsnouslevermaintenant _____

2. jevaisenvacancesdemain _____

3. monpetitfrèreapprendàlireetécrire _____

4. ilsaitdéjàécriresonnom _____

4 🖉

Change these verbs into the indicated plural form.

1. je dors, nous _____

2. je vais, nous _____

3. tu viens, vous _____

4. tu dis, vous _____

5. il prend, ils _____

5 🖉

Change these sentences around by using the pronouns given in parentheses; write the new sentences in the blanks. Example:
Je pars en vacances (nous) ▷ Nous partons en vacances.

1. J'entends la mer! (nous)

_____

2. Je dois conduire, je ne peux pas boire. (nous)

_____

3. Tu te lèves à sept heures pour aller à la plage. (nous)

_____

4. Tu veux du vin? (vous)

_____

5. Il peut entendre la mer. (ils)

_____

6. Il sait nager. (ils)

_____

1

C'est la grève! There is a strike in Paris. Now how will Julien and his wife Mathilde get to work without public transportation?

Read aloud the questions that Mathilde asks Julien, making sure that the intonation—that is, your voice within the questions—rises. You can also listen to the sentences on the CD.

1. Est-ce qu'il y a des métros?
2. Est-ce qu'il y des bus?
3. On prend la voiture?
4. On y va à pied?
5. Comment est-ce que nous allons au travail?

2

Because there really is a strike in Paris and all of Julien's answers to his wife's questions about means of transportation are negative, you can become acquainted with negation.

But be careful: In the confusion of the strike, Julien's answers to his wife Mathilde's questions have gotten out of order.

Connect the answers on the right with the appropriate questions on the left. You can also listen to the answers in the correct sequence on the CD.

1. Est-ce qu'il y a des métros?	a. Non, il n'y a pas de bus.
2. Est-ce qu'il y a des bus?	b. Non, on n'y va pas à pied.
3. Est-ce qu'on prend la voiture?	c. Non, il n'y a pas de métro.
4. Est-ce qu'on y va à pied?	d. On ne travaille pas! C'est la grève!
5. Comment est-ce que nous allons au travail?	e. Non, on ne prend pas la voiture.

3

The intonation question is frequently used in spoken French. It is constructed just like a declarative sentence, but the intonation rises to form a question.

> **Tu prends le métro?**

You can also ask a question by putting the expression **est-ce que** in front of a declarative sentence. Here too the intonation rises:

> **Est-ce que tu prends le métro?**

Before a vowel or a mute **h**, **est-ce que** is shortened to **est-ce qu'**:

> **Est-ce qu'il y a des bus?**

These are yes/no questions that can be answered either with **oui** or **non**. The expression **est-ce que** can also be combined with other question words, including questions in which the question refers to only a part of the sentence:

Comment est-ce que nous allons au travail? Nous y allons en voiture.

4

Julien wants to give his wife a small surprise for her birthday. He goes to a travel agency and finds out about several travel opportunities.
Look at the questions that the employee asks Julien. Match up the questions with the correct answers. You can listen to the entire dialogue on the CD.

1. Est-ce que vous voulez partir en avion?
2. Est-ce que vous voulez seulement des billets d'avion ou aussi un hôtel?
3. Est-ce que vous voulez partir en France ou à l'étranger?
4. Est-ce que vous avez déjà une idée pour le pays?
5. Est-ce que vous connaissez Venise?
6. C'est votre premier voyage en Italie?

a. Je préfère une offre avec avion et hôtel.
b. Non, je n'ai aucune idée.
c. Non, je ne connais pas Venise.
d. Oui, je veux partir en avion.
e. Je préfère aller dans un pays étranger.
f. Non, je connais déjà Rome et Florence.

1. _____ 2. _____ 3. _____

4. _____ 5. _____ 6. _____

5 ✏️

Complete these questions with the correct question words. You will find help in the **Bon à savoir** box.

1. _____ est-ce que tu pars? En Corse.

2. _____ est-ce que tu pars? En avion.

3. Tu pars _____? Une semaine.

4. _____ est-ce que tu pars? Parce que c'est mon anniversaire.

As you can see, the interrogative expression **est-ce que** is used very frequently in combination with question words: question word + **est-ce que** + declarative sentence:

Quand est-ce que tu pars en vacances?

The completion question (which can't be answered with **oui / non**) is also used in spoken French without **est-ce que**:

Tu pars quand? – Tu pars où?

6 ✏️

The question word **qui** always refers to a person. At the beginning of a sentence, **Qui . . .** corresponds to *Who . . .?*

Qui est là? – Qui prend le métro?

For the question *Whom . . .?* the expression **est-ce que** must be added:

Qui est-ce qu'on invite?

Qui est-ce que tu emmènes à la gare?

If you want to ask *To / for whom . . .?*, the preposition **à** is simply placed before the interrogative pronoun.

À qui est-ce que tu parles?

À qui est-ce qu'elle prête son vélo?

The question word **que** always refers to an object. Before a vowel or a mute **h** it contracts to **qu'**. In this case you can

- add the expression **est-ce que**:

Qu'est-ce que tu fais? – Qu'est-ce qu'on emmène en vacances?

- simply use **que**, but mainly with inversion questions in short common questions:

Que fais-tu? – Que veux-tu?

Complete the questions with the appropriate question words:

1. _____ est là?

2. _____ on invite?

3. _____ on fait?

a. Qui est-ce que

b. Qu'est-ce que

c. Qui

Bon à savoir !

Some more question words:

quand? – *when?*

comment? – *how?*

combien (de)? – *how many? how much?*

combien de temps? – *how long?*

où? – *where?*

pourquoi? – *why?*

quel, quelle? – *which?*

à quelle heure? – *at what time?*

Bon à savoir !

Here too the inversion question can be used in elevated speech or writing:

Quand pars-tu?

Comment vas-tu?

Bon à savoir !

Quoi or **comment?** If you have not understood someone or want to express surprise over something you have heard, you can ask **Quoi?** (*What?*). However, it's much more polite to use the question word **Comment?** (*What?*) in this instance.

7

One evening Mathilde comes home and finds her husband in the hallway with two suitcases. Complete the dialogue with the appropriate question words.

Julien: Surprise! Nous partons en voyage!

Mathilde: Quoi? Mais _____ allons-nous?
Julien: A Venise!

Mathilde: A Venise? Mais _____?
Julien: En avion!

Mathilde: Et _____?
Julien: Ce soir!

Mathilde: Mais _____?
Julien: Parce que c'est ton anniversaire!

8

Madame Duval bought shoes a week ago and now returns to the store. Read the dialogue and check off the negation words. You can listen to the dialogue on the CD.

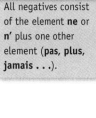

Mounir: Bonjour, Madame Duval! Vous voulez encore de nouvelles chaussures?

Mme Duval: Euh ... Non merci, je ne veux pas de nouvelles chaussures ... Mais je ne veux plus les chaussures jaunes de la semaine dernière!

Mounir: Oh, vraiment! Pourquoi?

Mme Duval: Eh bien ... elles ne sont pas très confortables! Et c'est un problème parce que je marche beaucoup, moi, vous savez, je n'aime pas prendre le métro ou le bus ...

Mounir: Ah, Madame, les chaussures, ça fait toujours un peu mal les premiers jours, mais ensuite, ça ne fait plus mal!

Mme Duval: Oui, mais ... elles sont jaunes ... et je ne porte jamais des vêtements jaunes!

Mounir: Mais, Mme Duval, vous pouvez porter d'autres couleurs avec ces chaussures! Vous n'avez pas des vêtements verts, rouges?

Mme Duval: Si, mais ... Je ne les aime plus, voilà!

Mounir: Ah, bon! Alors, dans ce cas, je ne peux rien dire! ... Et vous ne voulez pas les donner à quelqu'un?

Mme Duval: A qui? Je ne connais personne avec de petits pieds comme moi!

Mounir: Et vous ne voulez pas les échanger contre d'autres chaussures?

Mme Duval: Hm ... Je ne sais pas ... Qu'est-ce que vous me proposez?

9 👓

You already know one means of negation. It is the word **non**. In contrast to English, negation in French consists of two words: **ne** or **n'** before a vowel or a mute **h**, plus **pas**. Both elements surround the verb and any pronouns that accompany it:

> **Je ne sais pas. – Je ne veux pas de nouvelles chaussures.**
> **Je ne les aime pas. – Je n'en veux pas.**

ne ... pas can mean both *not* and *not any*.

This negation can be emphasized by substituting **aucun**, **aucune** for **pas**:

> **Je n'ai aucun pantalon jaune.** – *I have no yellow pants (at all).*
> **Je n'ai aucune idée.** – *I have absolutely no idea.*

Bon à savoir !

If you travel to France, you will notice that in informal speech, **ne** is frequently left out. However, it is required in writing.

10 👓 ✏️

Additional forms of negation:
- **ne ... plus:** as a contradiction to questions with **encore**:
  Est-ce que tu fumes encore? Non, je ne fume plus!
- **ne ... jamais:** often in answers with adverbs of time such as **parfois** and **déjà**:
  Est-ce qu'elle prend parfois le métro? Non, elle ne le prend jamais.
- **ne ... personne/personne ne:**
  Je ne connais personne.
  If the two elements of negation are used in reverse order, they do not surround the verb.
  Personne n'a des petits pieds comme moi.
  The word **personne** used alone and without an article means *nobody / no one.*
  Quelqu'un veut du vin? Non, personne.
- **ne ... rien/rien ne:**
  Je n'ai rien à dire.
  Rien ne va plus.
  Tu veux manger quelque chose? Non, rien, merci.

Bon à savoir !

After the negation elements **pas**, **plus**, and **jamais**, the indefinite and partitive articles are replaced by **de** or **d'**:
Est-ce que vous avez une voiture? Non, je n'ai pas de voiture!
Exception: After the verb **être** there is no change:
C'est un problème.
Ce n'est pas un problème.

Complete Mme Duval's statements with the correct elements of negation.

1. Mais je ne veux _____ les chaussures jaunes de la semaine dernière.

2. Je ne porte _____ des vêtements jaunes.

3. Je ne connais _____ avec des petits pieds comme moi!

4. Alors, dans ce cas, je ne peux _____ dire!

11

These questions and negative answers are scrambled. Put them back in the right order.

1. Est-ce qu' / métros / des / y a / ?

2. il / n'y a / Non / métros / de / pas / .

3. parfois / train / le / prenez / vous / Est-ce que / ?

4. Non, / ne / jamais / je / train / prends / le / .

5. au magasin / venez / vous / Pourquoi / est-ce que / ?

6. Je / veux / les / jaunes / chaussures / plus / ne / .

7. vous / les / plus / Pourquoi / ne / voulez / est-ce que / ?

8. Parce qu' / ne / pas / confortables / sont / elles / ne / .

12

Many people have a taste for adventure and are happy to just take off—Johnny, for example, who goes straight to Paris from Chicago, without having any specific plans . . .
But you can help him by completing the negative sentences. Write the correct element of negation in the appropriate blanks.

1. Il veut acheter un billet de métro. Mais il n'a _____ d'euros!

2. Il ne sait _____ où il va dormir.

3. Il n'a pas d'ami à Paris, il ne connait _____ .

4. Il va dans un hôtel. Mais il n'y a _____ de place!

5. Il veut aller à Montmartre. Mais il ne sait _____ comment y aller.

6. Il a un plan de la ville. Mais il ne comprend _____ , il y a trop de lignes!

7. Mais pour Johnny, _____ n'est un problème!

8. Et parce qu'il a toujours de la chance, il n'a _____ de problème!

> a. pas – b. personne – c. plus – d. pas – e. rien –
> f. jamais – g. rien – h. pas

13 🖉

There are a lot of people who don't like to travel and are not particularly fond of public transportation. Mme Duval is one of them. In this exercise you will see how she feels about this. Complete the sentences with the appropriate element of negation. Often there are several possibilities.

1. Je _____ pars _____ souvent en voyage.

2. Je _____ prends _____ l'avion, c'est trop cher!

3. Je _____ aime _____ prendre le train, le temps ne passe pas!

4. Je _____ aime _____ le bateau parce que là, je suis toujours malade!

5. Je me sens bien à Paris, je _____ ai _____ besoin de voyager!

6. Et dans Paris... Je vais à pied! Je _____ ai _____ de voiture.

7. Je _____ prends _____ le métro parce que je perds toujours mon billet.

8. Et à mon âge, on _____ fait _____ de vélo! Donc je marche!

14 🖉

Unfortunately, it is not always so easy to get from one place to another. Mathieu must travel to Château-Chinon on business for an interview. Susan, who comes from the U.S. and doesn't know much about transportation in France, asks him how he plans to travel. Complete Susan's questions with Mathieu's negative answers suggested by the illustrations.

Bon à savoir !
In France you have to pay to use the major highways. There are tollbooths known as **péages.**

Tu y vas en voiture? – Non, je n'y vais pas en voiture.

1. Les autoroutes sont gratuites?

   _____

2. Alors tu prends les routes nationales?

   _____

3. Alors, tu prends le train?

   _____

4. Alors, tu prends l'avion?

   _____

5. Mais tu as une autre idée?

   _____

15 ✎

Connect the questions on the left with the correct answers on the right.

1. Comment allez-vous?
2. Est-ce que tu vas bien?
3. Qu'est-ce que tu fais dans la vie?
4. Est-ce que tu as faim?
5. A quelle heure est le rendez-vous?
6. Est-ce que tu fumes encore?
7. Où allons-nous en vacances?
8. Vous partez en avion ou en bateau?
9. Quand est-ce qu'on arrive?
10. Quel âge a Mathieu?
11. Quelle heure est-il?
12. Tu préfères le train ou l'avion?
13. Qui ne vient pas ce soir?
14. Est-ce que tu vas parfois à la piscine?
15. Tu as encore des bonbons?
16. Est-ce que vous buvez de l'alcool?
17. Est-ce qu'il y a quelqu'un?
18. Est-ce que tu as quelque chose à manger?
19. Pourquoi est-ce qu'il n'y a pas de métro?
20. Quel temps fait-il en Corse?
21. Combien de bananes est-ce que tu veux?
22. Est-ce qu'il y a des métros?
23. Qu'est-ce qu'il y a à la télé ce soir?
24. Qu'est-ce que tu portes ce soir?

a. Non, je ne vais pas bien!
b. Je suis journaliste.
c. En bateau.
d. Il est 8 h.
e. Il a trente-et-un ans.
f. En Corse.
g. Marie ne vient pas.
h. Je préfère l'avion!
i. Non, il n'y a personne.
j. Il fait beau!
k. Il est à 15 heures.
l. Je préfère l'avion! Je porte une robe.
m. Non, je n'en ai plus.
n. Non, je n'ai rien à manger.
o. Parce que c'est la grève!
p. Non, il n'y a pas de métro.
q. Il y a un nouveau film.
r. Un kilo, s'il vous plaît.
s. Non, je n'en bois pas.
t. Non, je n'y vais jamais.
u. Je vais bien!
v. Non, je n'ai pas faim.
w. Non, je ne fume plus.
x. On arrive dans une heure.

1

Read the questions and choose the only logical answer.

1. Est-ce que vous aimez marcher?

   ☐ a. Deux heures.
   ☐ b. Oui, nous aimons bien marcher.
   ☐ c. Samedi, je vais au supermarché.

2. Tu vas au travail en métro?

   ☐ a. Non, en bus.
   ☐ b. Oui, en voiture.
   ☐ c. Je ne travaille pas le samedi.

3. A quelle heure est-ce que tu te lèves?

   ☐ a. Je me lève et je pars.
   ☐ b. Il est 15 heures.
   ☐ c. Je me lève à 6h45.

4. Comment est-ce qu'elle est, ta voiture?

   ☐ a. Non, je n'en ai pas.
   ☐ b. Elle est rouge.
   ☐ c. Oui, j'aime la voiture.

5. Tu pars combien de temps en Corse?

   ☐ a. Oui, je pars en Corse.
   ☐ b. Je pars deux semaines.
   ☐ c. J'y vais.

6. Avec qui est-ce que tu pars?

   ☐ a. Je pars avec ma copine.
   ☐ b. Je pars.
   ☐ c. Ma copine part.

2

Write the translations in the blanks next to the appropriate terms.

1. combien _____   6. qui _____

2. pourquoi _____   7. personne _____

3. comment _____   8. quoi _____

4. quand _____   9. rien _____

5. jamais _____

a. *why* – b. *how much* – c. *when* – d. *who* – e. *never* – f. *how* –
g. *nobody* – h. *nothing* – i. *what*

Negation

3 ✏

Marie and Thomas are brother and sister and don't agree about everything. Write the negative forms of the sentences in the blanks and start all sentences with the pronoun **il**.

1. Elle lit beaucoup. _____

2. Elle aime travailler. _____

3. Elle aime prendre le bus. _____

4. Elle fait du sport. _____

4 ✏

Write the missing elements of negation in the blanks.

1. Est-ce que tu prends parfois l'avion? Non, _____.

2. Est-ce que tu fumes encore? Non, je ne fume _____.

3. Tu connais quelqu'un à Paris? Non, _____.

4. Tu veux manger quelque chose? Non, merci, je ne veux _____.

5. Qui vient avec nous? _____.

6. Est-ce que tu veux dire quelque chose? Non, _____.

5 ✏

Which sentence matches each picture? Check off the correct sentence.

1. ▨ a. Il n'y a plus de place!
    ▨ b. Il n'y a personne!
    ▨ c. Je ne veux pas de bière.

2. ▨ a. Il n'y a rien dans le frigidaire.
    ▨ b. Il n'y a personne dans la rue.
    ▨ c. Il n'a pas d'argent.

3. ▨ a. Non, merci, je n'ai pas faim.
    ▨ b. Oui, merci, j'aime le vin!
    ▨ c. Je ne veux pas de bière.

4. ▨ a. Il n'y a rien dans le frigidaire!
    ▨ b. Il n'y a personne!
    ▨ c. Il n'a pas d'argent!

1

Julien and his family are newly arrived in Paris. He has been working for
a newspaper for a short while, and his wife has a job in a suburb of Paris.
Here you will learn about the "typical" daily routine of a French family.
Both parents work and the children are in school the whole day.

Unfortunately the order of events got mixed up. Put the sentences back into
the correct sequence, i.e., according to the time!

1. La famille se lève à sept heures.
2. Puis elle va travailler à Créteil de neuf à dix-sept heures.
3. Julien commence son travail à huit heures.
4. De midi à une heure et demie, c'est la pause déjeuner.
5. A quatre heures et demie, il va chercher les enfants à l'école.
6. Mathilde amène les enfants à l'école à huit heures moins cinq.
7. Il a des rendez-vous jusqu'à midi.
8. Le soir, ils mangent entre sept heures moins le quart
    et huit heures et demie.
9. Puis il va au bureau, jusqu'a seize heures dix.

Correct sequence: _____

2 TR. 36

Things sometimes get hectic in the morning at the Beauchamps's house,
especially because Julien's things are still in disarray as a result of the
move. Luckily, Mathilde helps him to find everything. Read their statements
and look at the illustration. Pay attention to the prepositions. You can
also listen to the sentences on the CD.

Ton appareil photo est sur le fauteuil.
Ton ordinateur est sous la table.
Ton téléphone portable est sur la cheminée.
Ton sac est devant le canapé.
Ton parapluie est derrière le rideau.
Ton agenda est dans ton sac.
Ta veste est dans l'armoire.
Tes clefs sont à côté de l'appareil photo.

3 TR. 37

As a photographer, Julien has to set up appointments. Sometimes this is not easy. Read the dialogue and pay attention to the times. You can also listen to it on the CD.

Nicolas M: Allô?

Julien: Allô, bonjour, c'est Julien Beauchamp. Nous devons prendre rendez-vous pour la photo...

Nicolas M: Ah, Bonjour, M. Beauchamp!

Julien: Alors, quand est-ce que nous pouvons nous rencontrer?

Nicolas M: Cette semaine, hmm... difficile! Je suis tous les jours au studio de huit heures du matin à huit heures du soir!

Julien: Et la semaine prochaine, vous avez le temps?

Nicolas M: En début de semaine seulement. A partir de mercredi, je suis à Bordeaux!

Julien: Bon... alors lundi?

Nicolas M: Un moment, je regarde mon agenda... Ah, lundi, j'ai un rendez-vous chez le coiffeur à quinze heures quinze!

Julien: Je peux venir le matin, alors?

Nicolas M: Euh... je préfère faire les photos après mon rendez-vous chez le coiffeur! Vous pouvez venir vers seize heures quarante-cinq?

Julien: Non, je suis désolé, je dois aller chercher mes enfants à l'école...

Nicolas M: Bon... et mardi?

Julien: Mardi... J'ai un rendez-vous à huit heures trente et un autre l'après-midi, à quinze heures. Mais je peux venir entre les deux, disons vers onze heures...

Nicolas M: Mardi, onze heures... Oui, c'est parfait! Vous avez mon adresse?

Julien: Non...

Nicolas M: 34, rue des Marronniers, au Pré-Saint-Gervais. Vous savez où c'est?

Julien: Non, mais j'ai un plan de la ville!

Nicolas M: Bon... A mardi prochain alors!

Julien: A mardi, au revoir!

4

Look at the illustrations of the time and fill in the blanks with the correct letters for the time. You will find help in the **Bon à savoir** box.

a. une heure   b. onze heures cinq   c. neuf heures vingt-cinq
d. une heure et demie   e. midi   f. midi et demie   g. trois heures
h. cinq heures et quart   i. sept heures moins le quart
j. onze heures moins dix

5

Johnny is an American visiting Lyon. The clerk at the hotel reception desk gives him some useful information. Look at his statements and write the times in the corresponding blanks. You can also listen to the sentences on the CD.

1. Nous servons le petit-déjeuner de sept heures à neuf heures quinze.
2. Le musée des Beaux-Arts ouvre à dix heures trente.
3. Il y a une visite guidée en anglais à onze heures moins le quart.
4. Beaucoup de magasins ferment à midi.
5. La pause de midi dure jusqu'à quatorze heures trente.
6. Entre seize heures et dix-sept heures trente, vous pouvez prendre un goûter à la française.
7. Le soir, les restaurants servent à partir de dix-neuf heures trente.
8. Il y a des métros jusqu'à minuit et demie.

1. _____   2. _____   3. _____   4. _____

5. _____   6. _____   7. _____   8. _____

Bon à savoir !

To tell the time, you say:
Il est sept heures –
It is seven o'clock, or
à sept heures – *at seven o'clock*
The hours are counted from 1 through 11 and the minutes are added on:
sept heures dix –
ten past seven.

To specify the half and quarter hours, the terms **et demie** or **et quart** are added to the whole hour:
sept heures et demie – *seven-thirty / half-past seven*
sept heures et quart – *seven-fifteen / quarter past seven*
However, when the quarter hour is subtracted from the next complete hour, we say **moins le quart**:
sept heures moins le quart – *quarter to seven.*

It is also possible to add **du matin** – *in the morning,* **de l'après-midi** – *in the afternoon,* **du soir** – *in the evening* to the complete hour.

Special cases:
midi – *noon*
minuit – *midnight*
une heure du matin – *one o'clock in the morning*

6

Madame Duval is retired. Her daily routine follows a set schedule. Read
the text and pay attention to the prepositions **à**, **pendant**, **après**, **avant**,
jusqu'à, and **vers**. Then put the illustrations into the correct order. You
can also listen to the text on the CD.

Mme Duval se lève à sept heures. Elle fait de la gymnastique pendant
une demi-heure. Après la gymnastique, elle se lave et s'habille. Il
est huit heures moins le quart. Elle prend son petit-déjeuner jusqu'à
huit heures et quart. Vers neuf heures, son chat arrive, elle lui donne
à manger. Puis elle fait des courses, avant le déjeuner, jusqu'à midi.

Correct order: _____

7 👓

One morning Madame Duval's cat doesn't come to breakfast. She looks for
it everywhere in the apartment. Where does she check? In searching for
the cat you will also learn the most important prepositions of location.

sur le lit   sous le lit   dans l'armoire   devant son
assiette

derrière le
rideau   entre les
fauteuils   à côté du
radiateur

8 ✎

Cats love to hide so they can sleep in peace. And in every house there are plenty of places for taking a catnap. Look at the pictures and select the locations where cats like to hide. Check off the correct answers.

☐ a. devant l'armoire
☐ b. sous l'armoire
☐ c. dans l'armoire

☐ a. derrière la fenêtre
☐ b. devant la fenêtre
☐ c. dans la fenêtre

☐ a. entre les bouteilles
☐ b. sous les bouteilles
☐ c. derrière les bouteilles

☐ a. derrière le rideau
☐ b. sur le rideau
☐ c. devant le rideau

☐ a. sur le balcon
☐ b. derrière le balcon
☐ c. à côté du balcon

9 ✎

Fortunately, Nicolas Martin has waited for Julien. The photo session can begin. Where does the musician have his picture taken? Look at the pictures and write the appropriate terms in the blanks.

1. _____ le jardin

2. _____ sa moto

3. _____ la cheminée

4. _____ Jimi Hendrix

5. _____ ses deux guitares

Prepositions of Location

10 👓

When are the various prepositions of location used?

à: for specifying destinations or places of residence in general or in the abstract.
- **à droite**, **à gauche** – *right, left*
- with cities: **Mme Duval habite à Paris. Je vais à Paris.**
- with masculine country names: **au Portugal**, **aux Etats-Unis**
- with general locations: **à la maison**, **à la mer**, **à la montagne**

en:
- with feminine country names, provinces, and regions:
  en France, **en Normandie**
- in certain fixed phrases: **en vacances**
- with means of transportation: **en voiture**, **en train**

Bon à savoir !

Pay particular attention to the expression **dans la rue**. This doesn't necessarily mean in the street but may mean on the street.

dans: for concrete place designations
- with closed spaces: **dans la cuisine**
- with many regions and precincts: **dans le 4e arrondissement**

chez: for specifying locations that are referred to through people:
J'ai un rendez-vous chez le coiffeur. Mme Duval va chez la voisine.

de: provides origin, point of departure.
Johnny vient de Chicago, des Etats-Unis.

11 ✏️

Mme Duval can't find her cat. It must have slipped out of the house. Write the appropriate prepositions in the blanks. In cases where it's not clear which preposition to use, the English translation is given in parentheses.

1. Le chat n'est pas _____ la maison.

2. Alors, Mme Duval va _____ la voisine.

3. Elle va voir _____ le jardin, _____ *(behind)* sa maison.

4. Elle va _____ la boulangerie, elle va _____ le coiffeur.

5. Elle va _____ Café Rose. Mais personne ne sait où est son chat!

6. Elle regarde partout _____ la rue, _____ *(under)* les voitures.

7. Elle regarde même _____ les toits *(on the roof)*. Pas de chat!

8. Alors, elle revient _____ la maison, toute triste…

9. Minou l'attend _____ *(in front of)* la porte!

12

Some prepositions can be used to situate a thing or a place precisely or to describe a route.
Many of these prepositions are formed with **de**.

Note the following prepositions:
- **à droite de** – *to the right of*
- **à gauche de** – *to the left of*
- **au milieu de** – *in the middle of*
- **en face de** – *across from*
- **près de** – *near*
- **loin de** – *far from*

The preposition **vers** is not used with **de**. **Vers** has several meanings:
- direction: **Cet avion va vers le sud.**
- around, near: **Elle habite vers la place de la Bastille.**

> **Bon à savoir !**
>
> Don't confuse the two statements **aller à droite** – *to go to the right* and **aller tout droit** (*to go straight ahead*).
>
> If you want to specify a turn to the right or the left, use the verb **tourner à droite**, **à gauche**.
>
> Note also the expression **passer à côté de**—*to go by something*

13 ✎

Because Julien is new to Paris, he doesn't know his way around very well. At 11 o'clock he has an appointment in **Le Pré-Saint-Gervais**, and he has a map of the city. Unfortunately, he doesn't know that there is a demonstration in the **12e arrondissement** today.
Look at the map and complete the text by writing the correct prepositions in the blanks.

1. Julien part _____ boulevard Vincent Auriol.

2. Il passe _____ l'Hôpital de la Pitié, puis il va _____ le pont de Bercy.

3. Il va _____, vers le quai de Bercy.

4. Puis il va _____, dans la rue Rambouillet. _____ ici, tout va bien!

5. Mais _____ l'avenue Daumesnil, les problèmes commencent...

6. Il y a une manifestation _____ 12e arrondissement!

7. _____ une heure, Julien ne peut pas avancer.

8. Il arrive _____ Nicolas Martin _____ midi.

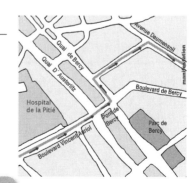

> à côté de – du – à droite – à gauche – dans – pendant –
> vers – chez – sur – jusqu' – à partir de

14

Johnny resumes his **Tour de France**. From Nice, where he has spent two days and will remain until the following day, he writes a postcard to a French friend in La Rochelle.
Write the missing prepositions in the blanks.

1. Salut Nadège! Me voilà _____ Nice _____ deux jours.

2. J'habite _____ un hôtel en face _____ la mer. C'est magnifique!

3. Je reste ici _____ demain.

4. Puis je pars _____ Marseille, _____ train.

5. Je reste là-bas _____ deux jours.

6. Après, je vais _____ la montagne, _____ les Pyrénées,

   près _____ l'Espagne.

7. Je vais donc bien sûr aussi quelques jours _____ Espagne!

8. Et _____ l'Espagne, je viens _____ toi _____ La Rochelle!

   _____ bientôt!

15

Look at the illustrations and check the correct time.

1
- a. une heure
- b. deux heures
- c. treize heures

2
- a. cinq heures cinq
- b. cinq heures dix
- c. cinq heures et demie

3
- a. huit heures
- b. huit heures et quart
- c. huit heures

4
- a. huit heures moins le quart
- b. huit heures et demie
- c. sept heures moins le quart

5
- a. une heure et demie
- b. une heure et quart
- c. midi

6
- a. deux heures et demie
- b. vingt heures quarante
- c. huit heures trente

1

Look at the times. Which illustrations do they match? Check the appropriate box

1. Il est six heures.

06:00   07:00   06:30

▓ a.   ▓ b.   ▓ c.

2. Il est deux heures et demie.

01:30   02:30   00:30

▓ a.   ▓ b.   ▓ c.

3. Il est sept heures et quart.

07:15   06:45   07:45

▓ a.   ▓ b.   ▓ c.

4. Il est cinq heures moins vingt.

07:55   05:20   04:40

▓ a.   ▓ b.   ▓ c.

5. Il est midi dix.

12:10   11:50   00:30

▓ a.   ▓ b.   ▓ c.

6. Il est minuit et demie.

11:30   00:30   12:15

▓ a.   ▓ b.   ▓ c.

2

Use numerals to write down the times shown in the left column.

1. sept heures du matin   _____

2. trois heures de l'après-midi   _____

3. neuf heures et demie du matin   _____

4. midi moins le quart   _____

5. dix heures et demie du soir   _____

6. une heure du matin   _____

3

Write in the blanks the French translations for the following prepositions:

1. *under*	_____	2. *on*	_____
3. *behind*	_____	4. *beside*	_____
5. *to the left of*	_____	6. *to the right of*	_____
7. *far from*	_____	8. *in front of*	_____
9. *after*	_____	10. *during*	_____

4

Johnny has his picture taken during his **Tour de France**. Which description corresponds to each picture?

à Paris,
- ☐ a. devant la Tour Eiffel
- ☐ b. sous la Tour Eiffel
- ☐ c. sur la Tour Eiffel

à Lyon,
- ☐ a. devant un restaurant
- ☐ b. à côté d'un restaurant

à Nice,
- ☐ a. sur un bateau
- ☐ b. derrière un bateau
- ☐ c. dans un bateau

à Marseille,
- ☐ a. dans l'hôtel
- ☐ b. à la piscine de l'hôtel
- ☐ c. dans la piscine de l'hôtel

à La Rochelle,
- ☐ a. devant un aquarium
- ☐ b. dans un aquarium

1

Look at the pictures and read what people did yesterday. Note the form of the verb in the past tense. You can also listen to the sentences on the CD.

J'ai travaillé au magasin de chaussures.

J'ai acheté des chaussures.

J'ai téléphoné à Mounir.

J'ai mangé dans un restaurant japonais.

J'ai dormi tout l'après-midi.

J'ai vu un film au cinéma.

Je suis allé chez le coiffeur.

Je suis allée au Café Rose.

2

Here you can read where and what various people ate and what they did afterward. Match up the sentence fragments on the left with the appropriate parts on the right. Then you can listen to all the complete sentences on the CD.

1. J'ai mangé un sandwich, puis

2. Tu as mangé une soupe, puis

3. Il a trop mangé, alors

4. Nous avons mangé en ville, puis

5. Vous avez mangé chez vous, puis

6. Ils ont mangé dans un restaurant chic, alors

a. tu as fait la vaisselle.

b. nous nous sommes promenés.

c. je suis allé au bureau.

d. vous êtes allés au cinéma.

e. ils ont payé beaucoup d'argent.

f. il a eu mal au ventre.

3

The passé composé is a past-tense form that is used to report what occurred in past time. Here's how it is formed:

> **avoir** or **être** in the present tense + past participle of the verb
> **J'ai mangé un sandwich.** *I ate a sandwich.*
> **Puis je suis allé au bureau.** *Then I went to the office.*

Fill in the blanks with the correct forms of **avoir** or **être** in the present tense:

1. tu _____ mangé – nous _____ mangé – ils _____ mangé

2. tu _____ allé – nous _____ allés – ils _____ allés

Note how the negative is formed: The second element of negation (**pas**, **plus**) comes right after the form of **avoir** or **être**.

> **Les enfants n'ont pas rangé leur chambre.**

4

Try to complete the sentences with the correct form of the participle. The basic form of the verb is in parentheses at the end of the sentence.

1. J'ai _____ mon enfance au Maroc. (passer)

2. J'ai _____ mes études en France. (finir)

3. Pour mon bac, mon oncle m'a _____ un voyage. (offrir)

> offert – passée – fini

Verbs ending in **-er** and **-ir** form their past participle regularly:
- **-er** verbs: The ending of the infinitive is replaced by **-é**.
  J'ai mangé des frites.
- **-ir** verbs (of the second and third groups):
  The ending of the infinitive is replaced by **-i**.
  Nous avons dormi tout l'après-midi.
  Verbs ending in **-vrir** (**ouvrir**) and **-frir** (**offrir**) form their past participle in **-ert**:
  Je lui a offert un cadeau; elle ne l'a pas encore ouvert.
  I gave her a gift; she has not yet opened it.

Bon à savoir !
Exceptions:
venir – *venu*
courir – *couru*

5 🖉

Look at the pictures and fill in the blanks with the forms of the verbs in the passé composé in the indicated person. You will find the basic forms in parentheses.

nous _____
(travailler)

vous _____
(jouer)

il _____
(nager)

tu _____
(grandir)

ils _____
(dormir)

6 👓 🖉

Most verbs form the passé composé with **avoir**, but some use **être**. These are verbs of motion or remaining:

aller, arriver, entrer, partir, rester, venir.
Thierry et Fatima sont allés à Marseille.
Mathieu et Raymond sont restés à Paris.

Verbs indicating means of motion form the passé composé with **avoir**:

marcher, nager, voler.
J'ai marché pendant une heure.

When the passé composé is formed with **avoir**, the past participle is the same for all persons:

Elle a mangé. Nous avons mangé.

When the passé composé is formed using **être**, the past participle agrees in gender and number with the subject of the sentence, much like an adjective:

Mathieu est allé au cinéma.
Marie est allée au Café Rose.
Ils sont allés au cinéma. Elles sont allées au cinéma.

Complete the following sentences with the correct past participle of **partir**:

1. Mounir, Thierry, et Fatiha sont _____ à Marseille.

2. Marie et sa grand-mère sont _____ en Normandie.

3. Susan est _____ en Angleterre.

> **Bon à savoir !**
> **avoir** and **être** in the passé composé:
> Both are constructed with **avoir**. The past participle forms are **eu** and **été**.
> **Mounir a eu son train.**
> **Fatima et Thierry ont eu de la chance.**
> **Il a été à Marseille.**
> **Ils ont été à Marseille ensemble.**

7

Mounir, Susan, and Marie return from vacation. They meet in the Café Rose and tell what their vacations were like. Read the dialogue and note the past-tense forms. Check off all the forms that are constructed with **avoir**. You can also listen to the dialogue on the CD.

Susan: Mounir, comme tu es bronzé! Où est-ce que tu es parti en vacances?

Mounir: Je suis parti à Marseille, avec mon oncle et ma tante. Il a fait super beau toute la semaine! Nous sommes allés à la plage tous les jours, et nous nous sommes promenés dans la région...

Marie: Et tu ne m'as pas écrit!

Mounir: Euh... Si, je t'ai écrit! Mais j'ai oublié de poster la carte!

Marie: Pffff... Moi, je suis allée en Normandie, il n'a pas fait très chaud, mais je me suis bien reposée! Et j'ai trouvé du temps pour écrire à mes amis, moi!

Susan: Tu es aussi partie en famille?

Marie: Oui, avec ma grand-mère. D'abord, nous sommes allées chez mes parents. Ils habitent à Rouen. Puis, ma mère, ma grand-mère et moi, nous sommes parties quelques jours à Honfleur... entre femmes!

Susan: Vous vous êtes bien amusées?

Marie: Oh oui! Nous avons beaucoup parlé... des hommes surtout!

Mounir: Ta grand-mère aussi s'est amusée? Elle m'a dit qu'elle déteste voyager.

Susan: Mais Mounir, tu connais la grand-mère de Marie?

Mounir: Oui! Elle est venue dans mon magasin deux fois. La première fois, elle a acheté deux paires de chaussures!

Susan: Oh, tu as réussi à lui en vendre deux! Bravo!

Mounir: Et la deuxième fois, elle a rendu une paire!

Susan: Ah...

Marie: Oui *(elle rit)*, elle me l'a dit. En tout cas, elle t'a trouvé très gentil! Elle m'a demandé de tes nouvelles, et elle m'a posé beaucoup de questions sur toi! Est-ce que tu as habité au Maroc, est-ce que tu as fini tes études...

Mounir: Ha ha, elle cherche un mari pour sa petite-fille!

Marie: Très drôle!...

> Il s'est promené. –
> Nous nous sommes
> promenés.
> Vous vous êtes bien
> amusées?
> Thierry et Fatiha se
> sont mariés en avril.
> Mounir s'est endormi
> dans le train.

8

The passé composé of all reflexive verbs is constructed using **être**. This means that the past participle agrees in number and gender with the subject.

9

There are a few irregular but very common past participle forms. Mark the ending of the participles that sound the same in these verbs.

1. Il a fait beau toute la semaine.
2. Si, je t'ai écrit.
3. Oui, elle me l'a dit.

Bon à savoir !

dire, **écrire**, and **faire** form their past participle by ending in **-t**.

- Formation of the past participle of most verbs ending in **-re**:
  The **-re** infinitive ending is replaced by **-u**:
  Et la deuxième fois, elle a rendu une paire!
  Exception: verbs like **prendre**, including **apprendre**, **comprendre**, and **mettre**, form their past participle by ending in **-is**.
  Vous avez appris la leçon?
  J'ai mis mon manteau.
- Verbs ending in **-oire**, **-oir**, **-aître**: the past participle ends in **-u**:
  boire – bu, croire – cru, pouvoir – pu, savoir – su, voir – vu,
  devoir – dû (with a circumflex), **vouloir – voulu,**
  connaître – connu, disparaître – disparu, and **lire – lu**.

Bon à savoir !

One further common but irregular past participle is **né**, *born*; it is the past participle of the verb **naître**. The passé composé is constructed with **être**:
Mounir est né le 26 août 1973 à Casablanca.
Marie est née en 1975 à Rouen.

10

Transform these sentences into the passé composé.

1. Tu parles. _____

2. Vous choisissez. _____

3. Je ne dors pas. _____

4. Nous attendons. _____

5. Elle y va. _____

6. Ils ne sortent pas. _____

11

Mounir is telling Mme Duval what he has done in life. The sentences are scrambled. Put them back in the correct order.

1. Je / né / suis / à / Casablanca / .
2. J' / ai / huit / habité / y / ans / .
3. En 1983, / sont / en France / mes parents / venus / .
4. Ma sœur et moi, / sommes / nous / à l'école française / allés / .
5. J' / eu / mon bac / 1992 / en / ai / .
6. Puis / étudié / à l'université / j' / ai / l'informatique / .

12

Which verbs form the passé composé with **être** and which with **avoir**?
Write the verbs in the infinitive form in the correct columns.

with **avoir**	with **être**

téléphoner – aller – rester – avoir – partir – courir – venir –
manger – faire – promener

13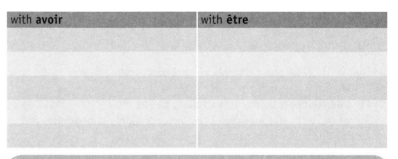

Mounir, Marie, and Susan are in the Café Rose. When Mathieu arrives, they
all tell what they did on vacation. Choose the correct past participle forms
in the following sentences. You can also listen to them on the CD.

1. Et toi, Susan, tu es *aller / allé / allée* en Angleterre?

2. Oui! Et la famille de Julien est *venu / venue / venus* me voir.

3. Ils sont *resté / restés / restées* deux jours chez moi puis ils sont
   parti / partis / parties en Ecosse.

4. Et toi, Mathieu, tu es *parti / partis / partie?*

5. Non, je suis *rester / resté / restée* à Paris, et Raymond aussi…
   Nous avons *travailler / travaillé / travaille!*

6. Oh, vous n'avez pas *eu / ai / eux* de vacances?

7. Si, mais en avril déjà! En tout cas, nous nous sommes bien
   amusés / amusé / amusées à Paris.

8. Nous sommes *sorti / sortis / sorties* dans des bars… et nous
   avons *faite / faites / fait* la connaissance de deux Suédoises!

14 ✏

Look at the pictures and fill in the blanks with the correct form of the verb in the passé composé. The infinitives of the verbs are provided in parentheses.

J'ai _____ un gâteau. (faire)

Il _____ tout le gâteau. (manger)

J' _____ la vaisselle. (laver)

Je _____ dans un bar. (aller)

J' _____ deux bières. (boire)

J' _____ deux heures! (dormir)

15 ✏

Mathilde meets an old friend in Paris, Catherine, with whom she studied. First Catherine tells about the years that have gone by, and then she asks about Mathilde and her family.

Write in the blanks the passé composé of the verbs provided.

1. J' _____ mes études (finir), puis je _____ au Canada (partir).

2. Je n' _____ pas la France pendant 12 ans (voir)!

3. Et cette année, enfin, j' _____ vraiment _____ venir (vouloir).

4. J' _____ des vacances, et me voilà à Paris! (prendre)

5. Et toi, qu'est-ce que tu _____ (devenir)? Comment va ta petite

   famille?

6. Bien! Julien _____ du travail à Paris (trouver), et nous _____

   ici (venir).

Bon à savoir !

When the expression **il y a** is placed before an expression of time, it does not mean *there is / there are*:

Nous sommes arrivés il y a deux mois. *We arrived two months ago.*

16 ✎

Look at the groups of terms. In each group, one word is not a past participle. Put an X by it.

1. ▨ a. fini
   ▨ b. couru
   ▨ c. choisi
   ▨ d. ami

2. ▨ a. joli
   ▨ b. grandi
   ▨ c. dormi
   ▨ d. parti

3. ▨ a. attendu
   ▨ b. du
   ▨ c. su
   ▨ d. pu

4. ▨ a. cru
   ▨ b. bu
   ▨ c. dû
   ▨ d. tu

5. ▨ a. mis
   ▨ b. pris
   ▨ c. appris
   ▨ d. gris

6. ▨ a. partis
   ▨ b. sortis
   ▨ c. venus
   ▨ d. pastis

7. ▨ a. lit
   ▨ b. dit
   ▨ c. fait
   ▨ d. écrit

8. ▨ a. parlé
   ▨ b. télé
   ▨ c. né
   ▨ d. travaillé

9. ▨ a. acheté
   ▨ b. allé
   ▨ c. olé
   ▨ d. été

10. ▨ a. rendu
    ▨ b. rosé
    ▨ c. fait
    ▨ d. sorti

11. ▨ a. allée
    ▨ b. année
    ▨ c. amusée
    ▨ d. arrivée

12. ▨ a. vert
    ▨ b. ouvert
    ▨ c. offert
    ▨ d. voulu

13. ▨ a. mardi
    ▨ b. chanté
    ▨ c. appris
    ▨ d. vu

14. ▨ a. rendu
    ▨ b. connu
    ▨ c. eu
    ▨ d. bleu

15. ▨ a. prix
    ▨ b. acheté
    ▨ c. vendu
    ▨ d. payé

The Passé Composé

1 🖋

Write in the blanks the past participles of the verbs provided.

    1. parler   _____

    2. avoir   _____

    3. finir   _____

    4. venir   _____

    5. rendre   _____

    6. prendre   _____

2 🖋

Is the passé composé of these verbs constructed with **avoir** or **être**?
Underline the correct form.

    1. Mounir *a / est* parti à Marseille avec Thierry et Fatiha.

    2. Ils *ont / sont* restés une semaine là-bas.

    3. Il *a / est* fait très beau.

    4. Ils *ont / sont* allés à la plage, ils *ont / sont* nagé.

    5. Ils se *ont / sont* promenés dans la région.

    6. Mounir n' *a / est* pas pu écrire à Marie.

    7. Il n' *a / est* pas eu le temps. Ou alors... il n'y *a /est* pas pensé!

The Passé Composé

3 🖉

Write the verbs provided in the blanks in the passé composé.

1. faire   Julien _____ des étude de technique, Mathilde de biologie.

2. se marier   Ils _____ après leurs études.

3. naître, avoir   Un an après, Chloë _____ . Puis ils _____ un deuxième enfant, Jonas.

4. rester, devoir   Ils _____ à Perpignan encore 8 ans. Puis ils _____ partir à Paris.

5. trouver   Julien _____ un bon travail là-bas.

4 🖉

Change these sentences into the passé composé. Write the entire sentence in the blanks.

1. Nous finissons de manger.

_____

2. Elles viennent et elles partent.

_____

3. Je ne comprends pas.

_____

4. Il veut donc il peut.

_____

5. Elle va au cinéma et elle y dort.

_____

6. Elles s'amusent.

_____

1

Basketball meets running! Both people are trying to compete with one another, so you can prepare yourself for some comparatives of adjectives. Look at the picture and read the statements by the two people. Then match them up with the right person. You can also listen to the sentences on the CD.

1. Je suis plus grand que toi.
2. Tu es plus petite que moi.
3. Je suis peut-être moins grande que toi.
4. Mais je suis aussi sportive que toi!
5. Et je suis plus rapide que toi.

The runner:

_____

The basketball player:

_____

2

Mathieu and Mounir like to talk about sports, even if they are not very active themselves. Read the sentences, in which adverbs are used. Which statements belong together? Write the pairs of numbers and letters in the blanks.

1. Zinedine Zidane, il est très sportif!
2. Et toi, Mathieu, tu fais souvent du sport?
3. Non, pas vraiment. Heureusement, il y a une piscine près de chez moi et j'aime bien nager.

a. Non, rarement... Pourquoi? Tu es un sportif, toi?
b. Ben oui, évidemment! C'est son métier!
c. Donc j'y vais assez souvent!

1. _____ 2. _____ 3. _____

3

Jonas and Chloé are competing with each other. Look at the illustration on the left and read the dialogue between the two of them:

Jonas: Je nage plus vite que toi.
Chloé: Oui, mais tu cours moins vite que moi.
Jonas: Ce n'est pas vrai, je cours aussi vite que toi!

Comparative formation:

to express		
superiority:	**plus**	+ adjective / adverb + **que**
inferiority:	**moins**	+ adjective / adverb + **que**
equality:	**aussi**	+ adjective / adverb + **que**

The adjective agrees in gender and number with the noun that it modifies.

> **Mathilde est aussi sportive que Julien.**
> **Chloé et Jonas sont aussi sportifs qu'eux.**

The comparative elements **plus** and **moins** are also used:
- before past participles: **Il a plus joué que travaillé.**
- before nouns and with **de**: **Il a moins de chaussures qu'elle.**
- before designations of time or age, only with **de** and without **que**:
  Il a nagé plus d'une heure.
  Il a plus de 18 ans.

4 ✏

Look at the pictures and write in the blanks the comparative form of the appropriate adjectives given in parentheses.

1.  Le ballon de basket est _____
le ballon de football. (grand)

2.  Le jean est _____
le pantalon noir. (court)

5

Look at the two illustrations and read the statements by Jonas:

Je suis le meilleur nageur!   Je suis le plus fort!

Superlative formation: **le**, **la**, **les** + **plus** oder **moins**
> **Je suis le plus rapide!**
> **Chloé est la plus grande.**

A noun can often follow, at least with short, commonly used adjectives:
> **C'est le plus grand joueur. – C'est la moins bonne coureuse.**
> **Ce sont les plus lents coureurs du monde.**

Longer adjectives, however, come after the noun; in this case, there is a duplication of the article:
> **Ce sont les coureurs les plus rapides.**

The word to which the comparison refers is connected by the preposition **de**:
> **C'est le plus petit joueur de l'équipe.**
> **Ce sont les coureurs les plus rapides du monde!**

6

It's Carnival! Julien's family has dressed up like the Dalton Brothers.
Look at the illustration and decide if the sentences are true. Cross out
the sentences that are false.

1. Mathilde est plus petite que Julien.
2. Mathilde est moins grande que Chloé.
3. Jonas est aussi grand que Chloé.
4. Jonas est moins grand que Chloé.
5. Jonas est plus petit que Julien.
6. Julien est le plus grand de la famille.
7. Mathilde est la plus petite.
8. Chloé et Julien sont les plus petits.

7

Connect the sentences on the left with the correct translations on the right. You can also listen to the sentences on the CD.

1. Il est plus rapide qu'elle.	a. *She is faster than he.*
2. Il est moins rapide qu'elle.	b. *She is slower than he.*
3. Elle est plus lente que lui.	c. *He is faster than she.*
4. Elle est moins lente que lui.	d. *He is the fastest.*
5. Il est le plus rapide.	e. *He is slower than she.*
6. Il est le moins rapide.	f. *He is the slowest.*

8

People also play sports in the newspaper office where Julien, Mathieu, and Susan work. The teammates are organizing a little basketball game in which the women will play against the men. Julien calls Mounir up to ask him if he would like to play because the men are in the minority.

Read the dialogue and check off all the adverbs in the text that end in **-ment**. You can also listen to the dialogue on the CD.

Julien: Demain, nous organisons un match de basket avec l'équipe du journal... Les filles contre les garçons! Tu veux jouer avec nous?

Mounir: Oui, évidemment, je veux bien! Mais je ne joue pas très bien, tu sais! En tout cas, je suis moins bon que toi.

Julien: Oh, ce n'est pas grave, on ne joue pas sérieusement! C'est surtout pour s'amuser! Et puis... on joue contre des filles!

Mounir: Bon, si ce n'est pas sérieux... c'est d'accord! Qui joue avec nous?

Julien: Raymond et Mathieu... Raymond joue assez bien, il court très vite! Et Mathieu, euh... il est moins rapide que Raymond, et il joue assez mal... Mais il est grand, c'est déjà bien!

Mounir: Oui... Mathieu n'est pas très sportif... Mais nous sommes seulement quatre?

Julien: Oui, pour le moment... Il manque encore une personne. J'ai pensé à ton oncle Thierry, je sais qu'il adore le sport.

Mounir: Thierry? Oh là là, il est vraiment mauvais. Il n'y a pas de pire sportif que lui!

Julien: Ah bon? Mais... il parle toujours de sport!

Mounir: Oui, ben... Il en fait rarement! ... Les gens qui en parlent le plus en font le moins!

Julien: Bon, mais tu peux quand même lui proposer...

Mounir: Oui, naturellement... Je lui téléphone ce soir et je lui demande!

9 ✏

Many types of sports are **fatigant** (*strenuous, tiring*) and others are
ennuyeux (*boring*), and in addition there are several types of athletes.
Fill in the blanks with the French translation of the adjectives provided
in parentheses.

1. Susan fait _____ *(often)* du sport, trois fois par semaine.

2. Et ce n'est pas _____ *(only)* pour s'amuser.

3. Elle en fait _____ *(seriously)*.

4. Elle va _____ *(first)* dans une salle de sport,

   et _____ *(then)* à la piscine.

5. _____ *(there)*, elle peut nager _____ *(for a long time)*, pendant

   une heure.

6. Thierry, lui, il parle _____ *(always)* de sport, mais il en

   fait _____ *(rarely)*.

7. Les gens qui en parlent _____ *(the most)* en font

   _____ *(the least)*!

8. Mais... il aime _____ *(a lot)* jouer à la pétanque...

9. Ce n'est pas un sport _____ *(very)* fatigant!

10. Mais courir, ça, c'est _____ *(really)* trop ennuyeux!

11. Sauf à la télé, _____ *(naturally)*!

10 👓

Adverbs are used to describe the manner in which something is done.
A verb can also be clarified by an adverb. Adverbs are invariable and
usually come right after the conjugated verb:

> **Tu nages bien. – Tu as bien nagé.**
> **Elle parle couramment le français.**

Adverbs can also clarify adjectives or other adverbs:

> **Il est très fort. – Elle nage assez bien.**

Adverbs can also be used to clarify an entire sentence or part of a sentence.
This usually involves adverbs of place or time or adverbs that clarify the
speaker's position with respect to the statement. Then they come either
at the very beginning or at the very end of the sentence.

> **Ils sont restés une semaine là-bas.**
> **Aujourd'hui, je vais à la piscine.**

Adverbs of location::
ici – *here*
là – *there*
là-bas – *over there*

Adverbs of time:
aujourd'hui – *today*
demain – *tomorrow*
hier – *yesterday*
maintenant – *now*
toujours – *always*
souvent – *often*
parfois – *sometimes*
jamais – *never*
longtemps – *for a long time*
déjà – *already*
encore – *still*
d'abord – *(at) first*
ensuite – *then*
enfin – *finally, at last*
tard – *late*
tôt – *early*
bientôt – *soon*

Adverbs of quantity:
beaucoup – *lots, much*
trop – *too much*
assez – *rather, enough*
peu – *little, hardly*

11 👓

In French we must distinguish between adjectives and adverbs because they have different forms. For example, compare these two sentences:

Cette histoire est vraie.
Je suis vraiment plus grande!

Adverb formation: feminine form of the adjective + **-ment**

naturel, **naturelle** ▶ **naturellement**
seul, **seule** ▶ **seulement**

If the masculine form of the adjective already ends in **-e** or another vowel, **-ment** is simply added to the masculine form:

facile ▶ **facilement** – **vrai** ▶ **vraiment**

Adjectives that end in **-ant** and **-ent** form the adverb by ending in **-amment** and **-emment**:

courant ▶ **couramment** – **évident** ▶ **évidemment**

12 👓

Some adverbs get their meaning from corresponding adjectives but don't end in **-ment**. They are related in meaning, but have different forms. Look at the following examples:

C'est un bon nageur. Il nage bien.
C'est un mauvais nageur. Il nage mal.
C'est un nageur rapide. Il nage vite.

Adverbs can be used in the comparative, just as adjectives can:

Elle travaille plus sérieusement que son frère.
Il court le moins vite de l'équipe.
Je nage mieux que vous!

Special adverb forms:
- **bon, -ne** ▶ adverb **bien**
  Vous allez bien?
  Tout est bien qui finit bien. *All's well that ends well.*
- **meilleur, -e** ▶ adverb **mieux**
  Vous allez mieux?
  Tant mieux! *So much the better!*
- **mauvais, -e** ▶ adverb **mal**
  Il va mal.
- **rapide** ▶ adverb **vite** or **rapidement**
  Il va trop vite.

13 🖉

Adverbs are formed from adjectives. Write in the blanks the adverb form of the adjectives provided.

1. Le match a commencé depuis _____ (exact) trois minutes.

2. Marie est _____ (absolu) sûre que son équipe est la

   meilleure.

3. Mounir n'est pas _____ (complet) d'accord.

4. Fatiha ne joue pas très _____ (bon).

5. En tout cas, elle joue _____ (meilleur) que Thierry.

6. Lui, il joue vraiment _____ (mauvais).

7. _____ (final), Marie a raison, l'équipe des femmes n'est pas

   mauvaise.

8. Elles vont _____ (sûr) gagner!

14 🖉

The basketball game between the men and women in the newspaper office is in progress. And you are the commentator! Be very careful to distinguish between adjectives and adverbs.

1. Raymond court *vite / rapide*. Mais Susan est aussi *vite / rapide* que lui.

2. Marie est une *bonne / bien* joueuse, elle joue souvent au basket.

3. Tanya est encore *meilleure / mieux*, elle joue *meilleure / mieux* que tous les autres!

4. Mounir, lui, s'amuse beaucoup. Il ne joue pas *sérieusement / sérieux!*

5. Et Fatiha non plus n'est pas très *sérieusement / sérieuse!* Elle parle tout le temps avec Mounir!

6. Ah! Thierry a encore dormi. Il ne joue *vraiment / vrai* pas *bien / bon!*

7. Alors Fatiha lui dit: "Tu es le plus *mauvais / mal* de tous les joueurs!"

8. "Ce n'est pas *vraiment / vrai!*", dit-il. "Tu joues aussi *mauvais / mal* que moi!"

15

The women in Julien's newspaper office make up the team opposing the men. Unfortunately, everything has gotten scrambled. Help to clarify things on the women's team by putting the parts of the sentences in the right order.

1. Susan est / grande / et elle joue / au basket / bien / très / .
2. Marie est / plus / Susan mais / elle court / vite / petite que / .
3. Mathilde / la / moins / de l'équipe / est / grande / .
4. Mais elle / aussi / que / bien / joue / Marie / .
5. Fatiha / jamais / de basket / fait / n'a / .
6. Elle / moins / que / bien / joue / les autres / .
7. Tanya / la / forte / est / de l'équipe / plus / .
8. Elle / encore mieux / les / joue / garçons / que / .

16

In each group, cross out the word that is not an adverb.

1. arrondissement – évidemment – naturellement – vraiment

2. souvent – rarement – toujours – appartement

3. vraiment – marchand – maintenant – seulement

4. moment – sérieusement – lentement – facilement

5. souvent – maintenant – parent – mal

6. vite – enfant – souvent – rapidement

7. instrument – vraiment – méchamment – joliment

8. client – maintenant – rarement – bien

9. bien – mal – cent – vite

10. bien – mauvais – mieux – souvent

11. ingrédient – heureusement – maintenant – jamais

12. heureusement – évident – naturellement – souvent

13. vite – rapide – lentement – rapidement

14. facilement – vraiment – argent – complètement

15. meilleur – bien – mal – mieux

1 🖉

Look at the pictures and complete the sentences with the appropriate comparatives (**plus**, **moins**, **aussi**).

 1. Chloé est _____ grande que Mathilde.

 2. Chloé est _____ grande que Jonas.

 3. Julien est _____ grand que Mathilde.

 4. Mathilde est _____ grande que Chloé.

 5. Jonas est _____ grand que Mathilde.

2 🖉

Write in the blanks the adverb form of the provided adjectives.

1. complet _____

2. sérieux _____

3. naturel _____

4. vrai _____

5. évident _____

6. rapide _____

7. mauvais _____

8. bon _____

Adjectives / Adverbs

3 🖉

Look at the sentences. Underline the correct adjective or adverb.

1. La famille de Julien est *vrai / vraie / vraiment* une famille de sportifs.

2. Le petit Jonas nage *rapide / vite / rapides* et *bon / bonne / bien*.

3. Sa sœur Chloé est aussi une *bon / bonne / bien* sportive.

4. Mais elle est moins *rapide / vite / rapidement* que son petit frère!

5. Par contre, elle est plus *grande / grand / grandement* que lui.

6. C'est *normal / normale / normalement*, elle a 14 ans!

7. *Evident / Evidente / Evidemment*, leur mère Mathilde nage encore
   mieux qu'eux.

8. Elle fait du sport *sérieux / sérieuse / sérieusement*, deux fois
   par semaine.

4 🖉

Complete the sentences using **bon**, **bien**, **meilleur**, or **mieux**. Don't forget
to make the adjectives **bon** and **meilleur** agree.

1. Thierry et Fatiha ne sont pas de _____ joueurs de basket.

2. Thierry aime _____ le basket, mais seulement à la télé!

3. Mais il est un très _____ joueur de pétanque.

4. Il est _____ que Mounir.

5. Et Mounir n'est pas content de jouer moins _____ que son oncle.

6. Et sa tante aussi est _____ que lui!

7. "Vous jouez _____ que moi, parce que vous jouez plus souvent!"

1

What's going to happen to Susan, Mounir, and the others? Read the following sentences to find out. At the same time you can get a glimpse into the future. You can also listen to the sentences on the CD.

1. Susan va rentrer en Angleterre.
2. Julien ne va pas partir.
3. Mathieu aussi va rester à Paris.
4. Mounir va s'installer en Belgique.
5. Et Marie, qu'est-ce qu'elle va faire?

2

The forms of the future are often used with various designations of time. Match up the time expressions on the top with the appropriate sentences below. The pictures will help you. You can also listen to the sentences on the CD.

1. La semaine prochaine,

2. Cet après-midi,

3. Le 14 juillet,

4. Dans quelques minutes,

5. Un jour,

a. je vais aller au Louvre.

b. le train va partir.

c. ils vont être célèbres.

d. elle va partir en vacances.

e. nous allons faire une fête.

1. _____

2. _____

3. _____

4. _____

5. _____

3 🖉

In French the future is constructed with the verb **aller**. In the sentences below, the personal pronouns are missing. Look at the verb forms of **aller** and fill in the blanks.

1. Je _____.

2. Tu _____.

3. Elle _____.

4. Vous _____!

5. Ils _____.

a. vas rester à Paris   b. va rentrer en Angleterre   c. vont me manquer
d. vais travailler en Belgique   e. allez venir me voir à Londres

4 🖉

To build the tense of the **futur proche** (*immediate future*), we have to master the forms of **aller** in the present tense, for the **futur proche** is composed of **aller** + the infinitive of the appropriate verb. Practice the forms of **aller** and complete the sentence. The **futur proche** is also referred to as the **futur composé**.

1. Susan _____ rentrer en Angleterre.

2. Nous _____ fêter son départ au Café Rose.

3. Vous _____ lui faire un cadeau?

4. Oui, moi, je _____ lui acheter un livre de cuisine française.

5. Julien et Mathilde _____ venir avec des fleurs.

6. Et toi, qu'est-ce que tu _____ lui offrir?

7. Je ne sais pas encore... Je _____ réfléchir.

5

These sentences are mixed up. Put them back in the right order.

1. travailler / en Belgique / Il va / .   _____

2. Nous / allons / pas / partir / n' / .   _____

3. manquer / Ils vont / me / .   _____

In French the future is constructed from the present-tense forms of **aller** and the infinitive of the appropriate verb:

> **Mounir et Susan vont partir de Paris.**
> **Et toi, où est-ce que tu vas habiter cette année?**

This **futur proche** is used:
* for the immediate future: **Il va manger le petit four.**
* for wishes, plans, or decisions: **Nous allons rester à Paris.**
* for expressing good intentions: **Je vais arrêter de fumer.**
* for advice, requests, and orders:
  Vous allez venir me voir à Londres, j'espère!

The infinitive comes after the variable forms of the verb **aller**. Other things may come between them, though:
* the second element of negation in a negative sentence: **Je ne vais pas manger ce petit four. – Ils ne vont plus habiter à Paris.**
* The object pronouns, including the pronouns **y** and **en**:
  Je ne vais pas le manger! – Ils ne vont plus y habiter.
* short commonly used adverbs such as **bien**, **beaucoup**, **peu**...:
  Je vais beaucoup travailler en Belgique.

6

The verb **aller** is used for constructing the forms of the **futur proche**, but its first meaning is *to go*. Look at these sentences and decide if the sentences are in the future tense—then mark with a check—or if the verb **aller** is used in the sense of *to go*—if so, mark an X.

1. Le mois prochain, Mounir va partir à Bruxelles. 　▨
2. Je vais maintenant au cinéma, tu veux venir? 　▨
3. Je ne peux pas, je dois aller travailler. 　▨
4. Mardi prochain, nous allons nager à la piscine. 　▨
5. Elle va tous les jours nager à la piscine. 　▨
6. Moi, j'y suis allée hier. 　▨
7. Bonjour, comment allez-vous? 　▨
8. Qu'est-ce que vous allez faire cette année? 　▨

7

Soon Susan will return to England. She gets together with her colleagues Mathieu, Julien, and Marie in the Café Rose to say good-bye. Mathilde, Julien's wife, is also there.

Read the dialogue and pay special attention to the future-tense forms. You can also listen to the dialogue on the CD.

Mathieu: Ah Susan, tu vas nous manquer! Le bureau va être vide, sans toi!

Susan: C'est gentil, Mathieu. Vous allez me manquer, vous aussi! Et puis le Café Rose aussi va me manquer!

Marie: Ne t'en fais pas, Susan, nous allons nous revoir bientôt.

Susan: Oui… vous allez venir me voir à Londres cette année ou l'année prochaine, j'espère!

Marie: Ah oui, avec plaisir! Mais pour le Café Rose, tu vas devoir revenir à Paris!

Susan: Oui, bien sûr que je vais revenir! Pas seulement pour le Café Rose, aussi pour le petit marché de Bastille, pour le canal Saint-Martin… et pour vous voir, évidemment!

Marie: Est-ce que tu sais déjà quand tu vas revenir?

Susan: Oui, je vais sûrement passer quelques jours ici à Noël… enfin, avant Noël, entre le 17 et le 20 décembre, pour acheter des cadeaux "made in Paris"!

Mathilde: Chouette, on va faire les courses de Noël ensemble, alors! Ça va être super!

Susan: Oui, quelle bonne idée! Et Marie va venir avec nous, c'est une experte du shopping parisien.

Marie: Euh… je ne sais pas si je vais être là en décembre…

Mathilde: Ah bon? Ne me dis pas que tu vas quitter Paris cette année, toi aussi!

Marie: Et si! … Mon contrat avec le journal va se finir le 1er octobre, et je vais chercher du travail… en Belgique!

Mathieu: En Belgique! Mais… Mounir aussi, il va s'installer en Belgique, non?

Marie: Euh… si! En fait, nous allons nous installer ensemble.

Tous: Hein? Quoi?

Susan: Ah, ça, c'est vraiment une surprise!

8 ✐

Susan and Marie have stayed in the Café Rose; they are talking about when they will see each other again. The sentences in the conversation are mixed up. Put them back into the correct order.

1. Quand / nous / nous revoir / allons / est-ce que / ?

_____

2. Je / passer quelques jours / en décembre / à Paris / vais / .

_____

3. Tu / vas / ne / être là / et Mounir non plus / pas / .

_____

4. Mais vous / bientôt / à Londres / me rendre visite /allez / .

_____

5. Je / naturellement / à votre mariage / venir / vais / !

_____

6. Mais Susan, / nous / pas / n' / nous marier / allons / !

_____

7. Oh, mais si! / on / faire / une belle fête / va / Comme ça / !

_____

9 ✐

Mounir and Marie already imagine their future life. Look at all the sentences and complete them with the appropriate forms of the verb **aller.**

1. Marie: Mounir et moi, nous *vais / allons / allez* habiter à Bruxelles.
2. Mounir: Moi, je *va / vais / vas* travailler dans une entreprise d'informatique.
3. Mounir: Elle *vas / vont / va* chercher du travail comme journaliste.
   Elle *va / vais / vas* me faire des bons petits plats... hein, Marie?
4. Marie: D'accord, Mounir... Mais toi, tu *vas / va / vais* faire les courses!
5. Marie: Et le dimanche, nous *vont / allons / allez* nous lever tôt et nous promener!
6. Mounir: Ah non! Toi, tu *vais / vas / vont* te lever tôt...
   Moi, je *vais / vas / vont* me lever à midi, comme tous les dimanches!

10 ✏

Here you can see the plans that Mounir and Marie have for their new life together.

Write in the proper order in the blanks the appropriate forms of the verb **aller** and the basic form of the verb that follows.

1. Cette année, ils _____ _____ plus de sport.

2. A partir de maintenant, nous _____ _____ seulement des produits bio.

3. La semaine prochaine, je _____ _____ un régime.

4. On _____ _____ ensemble le dimanche.

5. Pendant les vacances, je _____ _____ de fumer.

6. Nous _____ nous _____ tôt.

7. Le matin, je _____ _____ à manger aux chats.

8. Nous _____ _____ deux enfants!

> vont – essayer – allons – commencer – acheter – vais – va – courir – aller – vais – allons – lever – arrêter – donner – allons – avoir – vais – faire

11 ✏

While the adults make plans and good intentions, the children dream about their future life. Complete the statements by Chloé and Jonas with the appropriate future form of the verb provided in parentheses at the end.

1. **Chloé:**   Moi, plus tard, je _____ me _____ avec un acteur célèbre. (se marier)

2. **Chloé:**   Nous _____ une maison au bord de la mer. (avoir)

3. **Jonas:**   Moi, plus tard, je _____ Superman! (être)

4. **Jonas:**   Toutes les filles _____ m' _____! (adorer)

5. **Mathilde:** Oui, oui, les enfants... Mais vous _____ d'abord _____ vos devoirs! (faire)

12 👓

Read the following three sentences and try to figure out the differences in meaning.

1. Un matin, le chat a disparu.
2. Le matin, Mme Duval fait les courses.
3. Ce matin, Mounir va partir en vacances.

- Indefinite article + specification of day or time ▶ indefinite point in time, usually in the future or the past.
  Un jour, elle va être célèbre.
- Definite article + specification of day or time ▶ repeated action.
  Le samedi, elle se promène au parc des Buttes-Chaumont.
  Le week-end, elle mange souvent au restaurant avec Marie.
- Demonstrative adjective + specification of day or time ▶ a segment of the current day or year.
  cette année – ce matin – cet après-midi – ce soir
- Days of the week with no adjective ▶ specification of coming day of the week.
  Samedi, je pars en Belgique.

13 ✏

Read the following sentences and pay particular attention to the modifiers of time specifications in bold print. Choose the correct translation of the indicated part of the sentence.

1. Ne t'en fais pas, Susan, nous allons nous revoir **dans trois mois**.
   a. *in three months*   b. *for three months*   c. *three months ago*

2. **Le matin**, Mounir est fatigué.
   a. *that morning*   b. *in the morning*   c. *this morning*

3. **Cet après-midi**, je vais aller au Louvre.
   a. *every afternoon*   b. *tomorrow afternoon*   c. *this afternoon*

4. Ne me dis pas que tu vas quitter Paris **cette année**, toi aussi!
   a. *every year*   b. *next year*   c. *this year*

5. **Le samedi**, il travaille.
   a. *Saturdays*   b. *next Saturday*   c. *last Saturday*

6. **Ce samedi**, il va à la plage.
   a. *Saturdays*   b. *this Saturday*   c. *last Saturday*

14 ✏

The meaning of a time designation can change depending on the modifier. *Every night* or *tonight?* Write the missing modifiers in the blanks.

1. _____ matin, je prends toujours le métro pour aller au travail.

2. Son anniversaire est _____ 22 mai.

3. _____ jour, je vais tout lui dire.

4. Je vais venir entre _____ 17 et _____ 20 décembre.

5. Tu vas quitter Paris _____ année.

6. Tu viens au cinéma avec moi _____ vendredi?

15 ✏

Every good-bye is difficult. Translate into French the English sentences you see on the left and that are commonly heard during good-byes. The first letter is provided to help you.

Au revoir!

1. *I'm going to miss you!* T... _____

2. *I will write you.* J... _____

3. *We will call!* N... _____

4. *I'll come back!* J... _____

5. *Until next week!* A... _____

6. *Until next year!* A... _____

7. *I'll miss you (pl.) too!* V... _____

8. *That will be super!* Ç... _____

9. *Where will you live?* O... _____

10. *What will you do?* Q... _____

11. *I'll give you my address.* J... _____

12. *Until tomorrow!* A... _____

13. *I'm going to miss her!* E... _____

14. *I will always think about you!* J... _____

15. *Good-bye!* A... _____

16. *See you soon!* A... _____

1 🖉

Write the missing forms of the verb **aller** in the blanks to make the future form.

1. Susan et toi, vous _____ quitter Paris.

2. Mathieu, Julien, et Raymond _____ rester à Paris.

3. Mounir et Marie _____ s'installer en Belgique.

4. Mais nous n' _____ pas nous marier.

5. Susan n'est jamais allée à Bruxelles, mais elle _____

   y aller en janvier.

6. Je _____ faire une fête pour mon départ.

7. Ça _____ être super!

2 🖉

Marie and Mounir are imagining their new life together. Choose the appropriate form of the **futur proche**.

1. Le dimanche, je vais *prendre / ai pris / prends*

   mon petit-déjeuner au lit.

2. Mounir veut *manger / va manger / à manger* avec ses collègues.

3. Nous *allons / allons avoir / avoir* deux chats.

4. On *les a appelé / les appelle / va les appeler* Nirvana et Cléo.

The Future / Time Designations

3 🖉

Change these sentences in the present into the **futur proche**.

1. Je vais au cinéma.   _____

2. Nous faisons les courses. _____

3. Tu prends des tomates.   _____

4. Ils sont contents.   _____

4 🖉

Look at the sentences. For each one there is just one correct translation. Check the right box.

1. *In the morning Madame Duval goes shopping.*

   ▢ a. Le matin, Mme Duval fait les courses.
   ▢ b. Ce matin, Mme Duval fait les courses.
   ▢ c. Lundi matin, Mme Duval fait les courses.

2. *Next week I'm going to the movies.*

   ▢ a. La semaine prochaine, je vais au cinéma.
   ▢ b. Cette semaine, je vais au cinéma.
   ▢ c. La semaine dernière, je suis allé au cinéma.

3. *We'll have a party this Tuesday.*

   ▢ a. Mardi prochain, on va faire une fête.
   ▢ b. Mardi, on va faire une fête.
   ▢ c. Le mardi, on va faire une fête.

4. *On Sundays Madame Duval goes to bed early.*

   ▢ a. Le dimanche, Mme Duval se couche tôt.
   ▢ b. Dimanche, Mme Duval se couche tôt.
   ▢ c. Dimanche prochain, Mme Duval se couche tôt.

1

Exercise 1
masculine: un serveur; un étudiant; Mounir;
un pastis; un journal
feminine: une serveuse; une étudiante; une bière;
une table; une chaise

Exercise 2
1. h.; **2.** d.; **3.** b.; **4.** e.; **5.** f.; **6.** a.; **7.** c.; **8.** g.

Exercise 3
masculine:
fromage – gâteau – matin – travail – serveur
feminine:
vendeuse – table – chaise – carte – française

Exercise 6
1. des tables; **2.** des pastis; **3.** des quiches;
4. des euros; **5.** des personnes; **6.** des gâteaux;
7. des cafés; **8.** des bières

Exercise 8
1. vendeuse; **2.** serveur; **3.** docteur;
4. professeur; **5.** actrice; **6.** employé

Exercise 9
Caroline: Je suis...
musicienne; employée; danseuse; actrice;
boulangère; photographe; dentiste
Pierre: Je suis...
boulanger; employé; acteur; photographe; musicien; dentiste; danseur

Exercise 10
1. d.; **2.** a.; **3.** c.; **4.** b.; **5.** f.; **6.** e.

Exercise 11
1. professeur; **2.** journaliste; **3.** architecte;
4. étudiant; **5.** serveur; **6.** vendeuse;
7. photographe; **8.** jardinière

Exercise 12
Susan; Londres; Mounir Belaoui; Paris; Maroc;
Casablanca; France

Exercise 13
1. Américaine; **2.** Suisse; **3.** Espagnol;
4. Italiennes; **5.** Marocains

Exercise 14
1. d.; **2.** c.; **3.** b.; **4.** b.; **5.** d.; **6.** c.

Exercise 15
1. d.; **2.** g.; **3.** h.; **4.** b.; **5.** c.; **6.** a.; **7.** e; **8.** f.

Test 1

Exercise 1
1. une amie; **2.** une employée; **3.** une professeur;
4. une photographe; **5.** une musicienne

Exercise 2
1. b.; **2.** b.; **3.** b.; **4.** a.; **5.** c.; **6.** a.

Exercise 3
1. animaux; **2.** bureaux; **3.** bars; **4.** Anglais;
5. Portugaises; **6.** joueurs de tennis

Exercise 4
1. b.; **2.** c.; **3.** b.; **4.** d.

2

Exercise 1
1. c.; **2.** a.; **3.** f.; **4.** d.; **5.** b.; **6.** e.

Exercise 3
1. suis; **2.** es; **3.** sommes

Exercise 4
1. ont; **2.** avez; **3.** avons

Exercise 5
être: es; est; sommes; suis; êtes; sont
avoir: avons; as; ont; ai

Module 2

Exercise 6
danser: je danse, tu danses, il/elle danse,
nous dansons, vous dansez, ils/elles dansent
choisir: je choisis, tu choisis, il/elle choisit,
nous choisissons, vous choisissez,
ils/elles choisissent

Exercise 7
1. f.; **2.** a.; **3.** d.; **4.** b.; **5.** c.; **6.** e.

Exercise 10
1. suis – es – est – sommes – êtes – sont
2. ai – as – a – avons – avez – ont
3. pense – penses – pense – pensons –
   pensez – pensent
4. agis – agis – agit – agissons – agissez –
   agissent

Exercise 11
1. Il est deux heures.
2. Les enfants ont deux ans.
3. Ils nagent bien.
4. Nous aimons skier.
5. Nous commençons le français.
6. Nous choisissons un plat.
7. Tu achètes un vélo.
8. Vous achetez des gâteaux.

Exercise 12
1. habitent; **2.** s'appelle, parle;
3. a, s'appelle; **4.** est; **5.** est; **6.** aime;
7. aime, mange; **8.** a, choisir

Exercise 13
1. elle danse; **2.** ils nagent; **3.** elles jouent;
4. elle réfléchit; **5.** il neige; **6.** c'est une piscine

Exercise 14
1. mangeons, avons; **2.** emmener, as;
3. reste, ai; **4.** regardent, a; **5.** nageons, est

Exercise 15
1. Je pense donc je suis.
2. Quand le chat est sorti, les souris dansent.
3. La nuit, tous les chats sont gris.
4. Tu manges comme quatre.
5. Il est dans les nuages.

Exercise 16
horizontal:
1. PENSES; **2.** FINISSONS; **3.** GRANDIS;
4. COMMENCEZ; **5.** AVONS; **6.** EST; **7.** APPELLENT
vertical:
8. ONT; **9.** NAGEONS; **10.** SUIS; **11.** AIME;
12. DONNENT; **13.** CHOISISSENT

Test **2**

Exercise 1
1. est; **2.** a; **3.** êtes; **4.** avez; **5.** a; **6.** sont;
7. est

Exercise 2
1. b.; **2.** a.; **3.** a.; **4.** c.; **5.** a.

Exercise 3
1. danser; **2.** finit; **3.** finissent; **4.** dansent;
5. danse; **6.** finir

Exercise 4
1. habitent; **2.** ont; **3.** s'appelle; **4.** est; **5.** est;
6. aime

Exercise 5
1. Ce soir, nous mangeons dans un restaurant.
2. Vous achetez beaucoup de CDs.
3. Elles appellent Pierre.
4. Ce sont des journalistes, ils commencent le
   travail.
5. Nous commençons le français.

3

Exercise 1
1. a.; 2. c., b.; 3. e.; 4. d.

Exercise 2
1. d.; 2. a.; 3. b.; 4. f.; 5. h.; 6. c.; 7. g.; 8. e.

Exercise 3
1. la; 2. le; 3. l'; 4. les

Exercise 4
1. la poste; 2. la banque; 3. le supermarché;
4. l'épicerie; 5. le journal; 6. les timbres;
7. les lettres, 8. la brosse à dents,
9. le dentifrice; 10. l'eau

Exercise 5
1. Le; les; 2. la, la, l'; 3. les

Exercise 8
1. une; 2. de la; 3. de

Exercise 9
1. la; 2. un; 3. L'; 4. la, un; 5. des, les;
6. un, la, le, l'

Exercise 10
Mme Duval: une
L'employée: une, la
Mme Duval: les
L'employée: la
Mme Duval: une, une
L'employée: l', le, la, le, l'
Mme Duval: un
L'employée: une, les, l', l', un, les
Mme Duval: L', le

Exercise 11
1. des; 2. une; 3. de; 4. une; 5. un; 6. le, le;
7. une, les; 8. la; 9. une, du; 10. le

Exercise 12
1. a or b.; 2. a or b.; 3. d.

Exercise 13
1. une; 2. de la; 3. du; 4. du; 5. du; 6. la;
7. les; 8. les; 9. la; 10. les

Exercise 14
1. de; 2. de; 3. de la; 4. de; 5. des

Exercise 15
1. c.; 2. b.; 3. a.; 4. g.; 5. d.; 6. k.; 7. h.; 8. f.;
9. i.; 10. j.; 11. l.; 12. e.

Test **3**

Exercise 1
1. e.; 2. a.; 3. b.; 4. d.; 5. f.; 6. c.

Exercise 2
1. une; 2. une, une; 3. des; 4. des, les; 5. les

Exercise 3
1. des; 2. des, des; 3. les, un; 4. des, des;
5. les, un

Exercise 4
1. a.; 2. c.; 3. a.; 4. c.

4

Exercise 2
1. e.; 2. a.; 3. d.; 4. b.; 5. c.

Exercise 3
1. ce; 2. cette.

Exercise 4
1. Cet; 2. ces; 3. ce; 4. cette; 5. ce; 6. ce

Exercise 5
1. cet; 2. cette; 3. ce; 4. cette; 5. ce; 6. cette;
7. ce; 8. cet

Exercise 7
1. b.; 2. a.; 3. c.; 4. c.; 5. a.; 6. a.

Modules 4 and 5

Exercise 10
1. C'est mon billet.
2. C'est ton dentifrice.
3. Ce sont tes chaussures.
4. C'est ma place.
5. C'est son tee-shirt.

Exercise 11
1. leur chien; 2. leur appareil photo / leur caméra; 3. leurs lunettes de soleil; 4. vos billets; 5. nos billets, notre / mon avion

Exercise 12
1. b – c; 2. a.; 3. a – c; 4. a – c; 5. a. b.

Exercise 13
1. leurs; 2. notre; 3. nos; 4. ses; 5. mon; 6. ton; 7. mes

Exercise 14
1. this airplane; 2. his / her airplane; 3. my sunglasses; 4. his sunglasses; 5. this suitcase; 6. his / her suitcase; 7. our airline tickets; 8. his / her airline ticket

Test **4**

Exercise 1
1. cet; 2. ce; 3. cette; 4. cette; 5. ce; 6. ces

Exercise 2
1. Oui, c'est sa valise.
2. Oui, j'emmène mes chaussures.
3. Oui, j'emmène mon pantalon.
4. Oui, vous emmenez votre chien.
5. Oui, c'est leur avion.
6. Oui, ils emmènent leurs lunettes.

Exercise 3
1. a.; 2. a.; 3. b.; 4. c.

Exercise 4
1. e.; 2. b.; 3. c.; 4. e.; 5. d.; 6. g.; 7. h.; 8. f.; 9. j.; 10. i.

5

Exercise 1
1. Je; 2. Il; 3. elle; 4. Nous

Exercise 2
1. Lui; 2. Elle; 3. vous; 4. Moi; 5. Eux; 6. toi

Exercise 3
1. J'; 2. Tu; 3. Il, elle; 4. Nous; 5. Vous; 6. Ils, elles

Exercise 4
1. Elle; 2. Il; 3. Je; 4. Ils; 5. Elles; 6. Nous

Exercise 6
1. nous; 2. Moi; 3. Elle; 4. Lui; 5. toi; 6. vous

Exercise 7
1. Toi, tu; 2. lui, il; 3. moi; 4. nous; 5. Vous, eux

Exercise 9
1. les; 2. le; 3. la; 4. les; 5. t'

Exercise 11
1. lui; 2. l'; 3. le; 4. l'; 5. lui; 6. les, m'; 7. leur, m'

Exercise 12
1. en; 2. y; 3. en; 4. y

Exercise 13
1. Marc et Marion y sont.
2. Demain, j'y reste.
3. Nous en mangeons.
4. Il y pense toujours.
5. J'en ai besoin.
6. Il y en a encore.

Exercise 14
1. Nous la trouvons jolie.
2. Il regarde la télé avec moi.
3. Ils te téléphonent souvent.
4. Il lui donne la main.
5. Elle lui parle.
6. Vous pensez à eux.
7. Je voudrais en manger.
8. Tu restes à la maison? Oui, j'y reste.

Exercise 15
1. l'; 2. l'; 3. l'; 4. y; 5. en

Test 5

Exercise 1
1. nous; 2. toi; 3. je; 4. moi; 5. eux; 6. lui; 7. il

Exercise 2
1. Oui, elle est là.
2. Oui, il l'appelle.
3. Oui, on lui téléphone.
4. Oui, ils sont là.
5. Oui, il les appelle.
6. Oui, on leur téléphone.

Exercise 3
1. y.; 2. y.; 3. en; 4. en; 5. en; 6. y

Exercise 4
1. b.; 2. b.; 3. b.; 4. a.; 5. a.; 6. b.;
7. b.; 8. b.; 9. b.

6

Exercise 2
1. f.; 2. c.; 3. a; 4. b.; 5. d.; 6. g.;
7. h.; 8. e; 9. i.

Exercise 3
1. Elle est grande. Ils sont grands.
2. Elle est blonde. Ils sont blonds.
3. Elle est heureuse. Ils sont heureux.

Exercise 4
1. vieux, vieil, vieille; 2. nouveau, nouvel, nouvelle; 3. beau, bel, belle

Exercise 5
masculine: b, g, h, i
feminine: a, c, d, e, f, j, k

Exercise 6
nouvelles, belles, petits, jeune, petite, bon

Exercise 7
1. des chaussures noires;
2. des chaussures rouges;
3. des chaussures oranges;
4. des chaussures vertes

Exercise 8
1. d.; 2. a.; 3. b.; 4. c.

Exercise 9
1. Madame Duval cherche de nouvelles chaussures.
2. Il y a des chaussures rouges et blanches / blanches et rouges.
3. Madame Duval préfère les petites chaussures noires.
4. Elles sont discrètes et élégantes / élégantes et discrètes.
5. Il y aussi une jolie paire jaune.
6. Ces chaussures sont jolies mais chères.
7. C'est une bonne affaire, je suis contente.

Exercise 11
1. b.; 2. a.; 3. c.

Exercise 12
The following statements are incorrect: **1**, **3**, **5**, **6.**

Exercise 13
1. nouvelles; 2. noire; 3. bonne, bons;
4. contente; petit; 5. bonne; 6. chère;
7. précise

Modules 6 and 7

Exercise 14
1. deux filles américaines; 2. de vieilles amies;
3. blonde, de grands yeux bleus, 4. Français;
5. bel, gentil; 6. petite, blonde; 7. sympa, longs,
8. grandes

Exercise 15
1. d.; 2. f.; 3. a.; 4. e.; 5. g.; 6. h.;
7. j.; 8. i.; 9. b.; 10. c.

Exercise 16
1. seize; 2. dix, 3. quatre-vingt-quatre;
4. soixante-douze

Test **6**

Exercise 1
1. pauvres; 2. première; 3. rêveur; 4. grosse;
5. longue; 6. grand; 7. nouvelles

Exercise 2
1. a.; 2. b.; 3. a.; 4. c.; 5. b.

Exercise 3
1. vieille; 2. jeune; 3. mauvais; 4. chères;
5. grands

Exercise 4
a. dix-huit; b. trente-six; c. quatorze; d. six;
e. soixante-dix-huit; f. cinquante-cinq; g. onze;
h. zéro; i. soixante-huit; j. quatre-vingts;
k. 28; l. 95; m. 13; n. 10; o. 47; p. 72; q. 100;
r. 2; s. 16; t. 39

7

Exercise 1
allez, allons, va, vais, allez, vont

Exercise 3
1. je vais – tu vas – il va
2. nous allons – vous allez – ils vont

Exercise 4
je pars, tu pars, il part, nous partons,
vous partez, ils partent

Exercise 5
1. b.; 2. a.; 3. h.; 4. c.; 5. d.; 6. f.; 7. e.; 8. g.

Exercise 6
The first, second, and third persons singular and
the third person plural resemble one another;
the first and second persons plural also resemble
one another.
1. attends, vous attendez; 2. il croit, ils croient;
3. je bois, nous buvons; 4. tu mets, vous mettez

Exercise 8
1. fais; 2. faisons; 3. font; 4. faites; 5. fait

Exercise 10
1. voulez; 2. voulons; 3. dois;
4. faut; 5. veux; 6. peux

Exercise 11
1. peut; 2. pouvons; 3. peux; 4. peut; 5. sait;
6. peux; 7. sais, peux; 8. savent

Exercise 13
1. nous; 2. me; 3. vous; 4. se; 5. te; 6. se, s'

Exercise 14
1. pars; 2. vais; 3. vient, dormons;
4. viens, viennent; 5. partez; 6. partons, part;
7. vais; 8. pars

Exercise 15
1. ils vont; **2.** il voit; **3.** elle veut;
4. il doit; **5.** ils disent

Exercise 16
horizontal:
1. PROMETTEZ; **2.** FONT; **3.** DITES; **4.** VAS;
5. VOIT; **6.** VEULENT; **7.** PREND; **8.** SENT;
9. CONNAIS; **10.** SAVONS; **11.** RIT; **12.** SORS
vertical:
13. OFFRENT; **14.** PEUVENT; **15.** ENTENDEZ;
16. VIENNENT; **17.** DOIS; **18.** TE; **19.** DIS;
20. LISEZ; **21.** BOIS; **22.** SAIT

Test **7**

Exercise 1
1. e.; **2.** a.; **3.** b.; **4.** h.; **5.** c.; **6.** d.; **7.** g.; **8.** f.

Exercise 2
1. g.; **2.** a.; **3.** j.; **4.** b.; **5.** f.; **6.** c.;
7. e.; **8.** d.; **9.** i.; **10.** h.

Exercise 3
1. Nous devons nous lever maintenant.
2. Je vais en vacances demain.
3. Mon petit frère apprend à lire et écrire.
4. Il sait déjà écrire son nom.

Exercise 4
1. dormons; **2.** allons; **3.** venez;
4. dites; **5.** prennent

Exercise 5
1. Nous entendons la mer.
2. Nous devons conduire, nous ne pouvons pas boire.
3. Nous nous levons à sept heures pour aller à la plage.
4. Vous voulez du vin?
5. Ils peuvent entendre la mer.
6. Ils savent nager.

8

Exercise 2
1. c.; **2.** a.; **3.** e.; **4.** b.; **5.** d.

Exercise 4
1. d.; **2.** a.; **3.** e.; **4.** b.; **5.** c.; **6.** f.

Exercise 5
1. Où; **2.** Comment; **3.** combien de temps;
4. Pourquoi

Exercise 6
1. c.; **2.** a.; **3.** b.

Exercise 7
où; comment; quand; pourquoi

Exercise 8
non merci; ne pas; ne plus; ne pas; n' pas;
ne plus; ne jamais; n' pas; ne plus; ne rien;
ne pas; ne personne; ne pas; ne pas

Exercise 10
1. pas; **2.** jamais; **3.** personne; **4.** rien

Exercise 11
1. Est-ce qu'il y a des métros?
2. Non, il n'y a pas de métros.
3. Est-ce que vous prenez parfois le train?
4. Non, je ne prends jamais le train.
5. Pourquoi est-ce que vous venez au magasin?
6. Je ne veux plus les chaussures jaunes.
7. Pourquoi est-ce que vous ne les voulez plus?
8. Parce qu'elles ne sont pas confortables.

Exercise 12
1. a.; **2.** d.; **3.** b.; **4.** c.; **5.** h.; **6.** e.; **7.** g.; **8.** f.

Exercise 13
1. ne, pas / jamais; **2.** ne, pas / jamais; **3.** n', pas;
4. n', pas; **5.** n', pas / jamais / plus; **6.** n', pas;
7. ne, pas / jamais; **8.** ne, pas

Answers

Modules 8 and 9

Exercise 14
1. Non, elles ne sont pas gratuites.
2. Non, je ne prends pas les routes nationales.
3. Non, je ne prends pas le train.
4. Non, je ne prends pas l'avion.
5. Non, je n'ai pas d'autre idée.

Exercise 15
1. u.; **2.** a.; **3.** b.; **4.** v.; **5.** k.; **6.** w.; **7.** f.;
8. c.; **9.** x.; **10.** e.; **11.** d.; **12.** h.; **13.** g.;
14. t.; **15.** m.; **16.** s.; **17.** i.; **18.** n.; **19.** o.;
20. j.; **21.** r.; **22.** p.; **23.** q.; **24.** l.

Test 8

Exercise 1
1. b.; **2.** a.; **3.** c.; **4.** b.; **5.** b.; **6.** a.

Exercise 2
1. b.; **2.** a.; **3.** f.; **4.** c.; **5.** e.; **6.** d.;
7. g.; **8.** i.; **9.** h.

Exercise 3
1. Il ne lit pas beaucoup.
2. Il n'aime pas travailler.
3. Il n'aime pas prendre le bus.
4. Il n'aime pas faire de sport.

Exercise 4
1. jamais; **2.** plus; **3.** personne; **4.** rien;
5. personne; **6.** rien

Exercise 5
1. a.; **2.** b.; **3.** b.; **4.** a.

9

Exercise 1
1. 6. 2. 3. 7. 4. 9. 5. 8.

Exercise 4
1. a.; **2.** g.; **3.** b.; **4.** h.; **5.** c.; **6.** d.;
7. i.; **8.** j.; **9.** e.; **10.** f.

Exercise 5
1. 7.00; 9.15
2. 10.30
3. 10.45
4. 12.00
5. 12.00, 14.30
6. 16.00, 17.30
7. 19.30
8. 00.30

Exercise 6
c. a. d. f. b. e.

Exercise 8
1. c.; **2.** b.; **3.** a.; **4.** a.; **5.** a.

Exercise 9
1. dans; **2.** sur; **3.** devant; **4.** à côté de; **5.** entre

Exercise 11
1. à; **2.** chez; **3.** dans, derrière; **4.** à, chez; **5.** au;
6. dans, sous; **7.** sur; **8.** à; **9.** devant

Exercise 13
1. du; **2.** à côté de, sur; **3.** à gauche;
4. à droite, jusqu'; **5.** à partir de; **6.** dans;
7. pendant; **8.** chez, vers

Exercise 14
1. à, pendant; **2.** dans, de; **3.** jusqu'à;
4. à, en; **5.** pendant; **6.** à, dans, de; **7.** en;
8. après, chez, à, À

Exercise 15
1. a.; **2.** b.; **3.** b.; **4.** a.; **5.** a.; **6.** a.

Test 9

Exercise 1
1. a.; **2.** b.; **3.** a.; **4.** c.; **5.** a.; **6.** b.

Exercise 2
1. 7.00; **2.** 15.00; **3.** 9.30;
4. 11.45; **5.** 22.30; **6.** 1.00

Exercise 3
1. sous; 2. sur; 3. derrière; 4. à côté de;
5. à gauche de; 6. à droite de; 7. loin de;
8. devant; 9. après; 10. pendant

Exercise 4
1. a; 2. c.; 3. a.; 4. b; 5. a.

10

Exercise 2
1. c.; 2. a.; 3. f.; 4. b.; 5. d.; 6. e.

Exercise 3
1. as, avons, ont; 2. es, sommes, sont

Exercise 4
1. passé; 2. fini; 3. offert

Exercise 5
1. avons; 2. avez; 3. ont; 4. as; 5. ont

Exercise 6
1. partis; 2. parties; 3. partie

Exercise 7
a fait, as écrit; ai écrit; ai oublié; a fait;
ai trouvé; avons parlé; a dit; a acheté; as réussi;
a rendu; a dit; a trouvé; a demandé; a posé;
as habité; as fini

Exercise 9
fait; écrit; dit.

Exercise 10
1. Tu as parlé.
2. Vous avez choisi.
3. Je n'ai pas dormi.
4. Nous avons attendu.
5. Elle y est allée.
6. Ils ne sont pas sortis.

Exercise 11
1. Je suis né à Casablanca.
2. J'y ai habité huit ans.
3. En 1983, mes parents sont venus en France.
4. Ma sœur et moi, nous sommes allés à l'école française.
5. J'ai eu mon bac en 1992.
6. Puis j'ai etudié l'informatique à l'université.

Exercise 12
with avoir:
téléphoner; avoir; courir; manger; faire
with être:
aller; rester; partir; venir; promener

Exercise 13
1. allée; 2. venue; 3. restés, partis;
4. parti; 5. resté, travaillé; 6. eu; 7. amusés;
8. sortis, fait

Exercise 14
1. ai fait; 2. a mangé; 3. ai lavé; 4. suis allé/ée;
5. ai bu; 6. ai dormi

Exercise 15
1. ai fini, suis partie; 2. ai vu; 3. ai voulu; 4. ai pris; 5. es devenue; 6. a trouvé, sommes venus

Exercise 16
1. d.; 2. a.; 3. b.; 4. tu; 5. d.; 6. d.; 7. a.; 8. b.;
9. c.; 10. b.; 11. b.; 12. a.; 13. a.; 14. d.; 15. a.

Test **10**

Exercise 1
1. parlé; 2. eu; 3. fini; 4. venu; 5. rendu; 6. pris

Exercise 2
1. est; 2. sont; 3. a; 4. sont, ont;
5. sont; 6. a; 7. a, a

Exercise 3
1. a fait; 2. se sont mariés; 3. est née, ont eu;
4. sont restés, ont dû; 5. a trouvé

Modules 10 and 11

Exercise 4
1. Nous avons fini de manger.
2. Elles sont venues et elles sont parties.
3. Je n'ai pas compris.
4. Il a voulu donc il a pu.
5. Elle est allée au cinéma et elle y a dormi.
6. Elles se sont amusées.

11

Exercise 1
The male runner: 3, 4, 5
The female runner: 1, 2

Exercise 2
1. b.; 2. a.; 3. c.

Exercise 4
1. plus grand que; 2. moins court que

Exercise 6
Incorrect sentences: 2, 3, 7, 8

Exercise 7
1. c.; 2. e.; 3. b.; 4. a.; 5. d.; 6. f.

Exercise 8
évidemment; sérieusement; vraiment;
rarement; naturellement

Exercise 9
1. souvent; 2. seulement; 3. sérieusement;
4. d'abord, ensuite / puis / après;
5. là-bas, longtemps; 6. toujours, rarement;
7. le plus, le moins; 8. bien; 9. très;
10. vraiment; 11. naturellement

Exercise 13
1. exactement; 2. absolument;
3. complètement; 4. bien; 5. mieux;
6. mal; 7. Finalement; 8. sûrement

Exercise 14
1. vite, rapide; 2. bonne; 3. meilleure, mieux;
4. sérieusement; 5. sérieuse; 6. vraiment, bien;
7. mauvais; 8. vrai, mal

Exercise 15
1. Susan est grande et elle joue très bien
   au basket.
2. Marie est plus petite que Susan mais
   elle court vite.
3. Mathilde est la moins grande de l'équipe.
4. Mais elle joue aussi bien que Marie.
5. Fatiha n'a jamais fait de basket.
6. Elle joue moins bien que les autres.
7. Tanja est la plus forte de l'équipe.
8. Elle joue encore mieux que les garçons.

Exercise 16
1. arrondissement; 2. appartement; 3. marchand;
4. moment; 5. parent; 6. enfant; 7. instrument;
8. client; 9. cent; 10. mauvais; 11. ingrédient;
12. évident; 13. rapide; 14. argent; 15. mal

Test **11**

Exercise 1
1. plus petite; 2. plus grande; 3. plus;
4. plus; 5. moins

Exercise 2
1. complètement; 2. sérieusement;
3. naturellement; 4. vraiment; 5. évidemment;
6. rapidement; 7. mal; 8. bien

Exercise 3
1. vraiment; 2. vite, bien; 3. bonne;
4. rapide; 5. grande, 6. normal; 7. Evidemment;
8. sérieusement

Exercise 4
1. bons; 2. bien, 3. bon; 4. meilleur;
5. bien, 6. meilleure; 7. mieux

12

Exercise 2
1. d.; **2.** a.; **3.** e.; **4.** b.; **5.** c.

Exercise 3
1. d.; **2.** a.; **3.** b., **4.** e.; **5.** c.

Exercise 4
1. va; **2.** allons; **3.** allez; **4.** vais;
5. vont; **6.** vas; **7.** vais

Exercise 5
1. Il va travailler en Belgique.
2. Nous n'allons pas partir.
3. Ils vont me manquer.

Exercise 6
X next to sentences: 2, 3, 5, 6, 7

Exercise 8
1. Quand est-ce que nous allons nous revoir?
2. Je vais passer quelques jours à Paris
en décembre.
3. Tu ne vas pas être là et Mounir non plus.
4. Mais vous allez bientôt me rendre visite
à Londres.
5. Je vais naturellement venir à votre mariage!
6. Mais, Susan, nous n'allons pas nous marier!
7. Oh mais si! Comme ça, on va faire une belle
fête!

Exercise 9
1. allons; **2.** vais; **3.** va, va;
4. vas; **5.** allons; **6.** vas, vais

Exercise 10
1. vont faire; **2.** allons acheter;
3. vais commencer; **4.** va courir; **5.** vais arrêter;
6. allons lever; **7.** vais donner; **8.** allons avoir

Exercise 11
1. vais me marier; **2.** allons avoir; **3.** vais être;
4. vont m'adorer; **5.** allez faire

Exercise 13
1. a.; **2.** b.; **3.** c.; **4.** c.; **5.** a.; **6.** b.

Exercise 14
1. Le; **2.** le; 3. un; **4.** le, le; **5.** cette; **6.** —

Exercise 15
1. Tu vas me manquer!
2. Je vais t'écrire!
3. Nous allons téléphoner!
4. Je vais revenir!
5. A la semaine prochaine!
6. A l'année prochaine!
7. Vous allez me manquer aussi!
8. Ça va être super!
9. Où est-ce que tu vas habiter?
10. Qu'est-ce que tu vas faire?
11. Je vais te donner mon adresse.
12. A demain!
13. Elle va me manquer.
14. Je vais toujours penser à toi!
15. Au revoir!
16. A bientôt!

Test 12

Exercise 1
1. allez, **2.** vont; **3.** vont; **4.** allons;
5. va; **6.** vais, **7.** va

Exercise 2
1. vais prendre; **2.** va manger, **3.** allons avoir;
4. va les appeler

Exercise 3
1. Je vais aller au cinéma.
2. Nous allons faire les courses.
3. Tu vas prendre des tomates.
4. Ils vont être contents.

Exercise 4
1. a.; **2.** a., **3.** b.; **4.** a.

Overview of Contents

1. Articles
2. The Verb *être*
3. The Verb *avoir*
4. 1st-Group verbs
5. 2nd-Group verbs
6. 3rd-Group verbs
7. The Verb *aller*
8. The Verb *s'asseoir*
9. The Verb *boire*
10. The Verb *connaître*
11. The Verb *croire*
12. The Verb *dire*
13. The Verb *faire*
14. The Verb *pouvoir*
15. The Verb *prendre*
16. The Verb *savoir*
17. The Verb *venir*
18. The Verb *voir*
19. The Verb *vouloir*
20. The Past
21. The Immediate Past
22. The Past Participle
23. The Immediate Future Tense
24. Modal Verbs
25. Reflexive Verbs
26. Impersonal Expressions
27. Pronouns
28. Noun Gender
29. Formation of Plural Nouns
30. Asking Questions
31. Demonstrative Adjectives
32. Question Words
33. Negation
34. Adjectives
35. Adverbs
36. Prepositions
37. Cardinal Numbers
38. Ordinal Numbers
39. Telling Time
40. Prefixes
41. Apostrophe

§ 1 Articles

Indefinite Articles

masculine

Singular:	**un nom**
	un apéritif
Plural:	**des noms**
	des apéritifs

feminine

Singular:	**une porte**
	une entrée
Plural:	**des portes**
	des entrées

The indefinite article always is the same, whether it comes before a word that starts with a consonant, a vowel, or a mute **h**. The indefinite article has only one plural form in French: **des** is used for both masculine and feminine nouns in the plural.

Definite Articles

masculine singular before a consonant: **le salon**
before a vowel or mute **h**: **l'océan**
plural before a consonant: **les salons**
before a vowel or a mute **h**: **les océans**

feminine singular before a consonant: **la chambre**
before a vowel or mute **h**: **l'entrée**
plural before a consonant: **les chambres**
before a vowel or mute **h**: **les entrées**

The masculine singular form of the definite article is **le**; the feminine form is **la**. Before a vowel or a mute **h**, **le** and **la** are shortened to **l'**. There are no neuter nouns in French, in contrast to some languages.
The plural of the definite article is always **les**.

The definite article is used after the verbs **aimer**, **adorer**, and **détester**. English commonly uses no article in such instances.

J'aime le fromage.
I like cheese.
J'adore les gâteaux.
I love cakes.
Je déteste les cornichons.
I can't stand pickles.

The Partitive Article

In French the partitive article (**du**, **de la**, **de l'**, **des**) designates an unspecified quantity and is used with things that can't be counted (for example, coffee, cheese, water, etc.). It is often not translated in English.
Laure mange de l'ananas.
Laura eats pineapple.
Il y a du beurre et de la brioche.
There is some bread and rolls.

Verbs such as **aimer**, **adorer**, etc., are an exception: They are not followed by a partitive article but rather by the definite article.

The partitive article is used after **avec**:
Nathalie aime le thé avec du sucre.

Sans is followed by no article:
Elle aime le café sans sucre.

§ 2 The Verb *être*

The verb **être** (*to be*) is irregular.

être

je	suis
tu	es
il /elle /on	est
nous	sommes
vous	êtes
ils /elles	sont

C'est + an adjective or **c'est** + a name is used in describing something or introducing someone.

>**C'est joli.**
>**C'est Laure, ma femme.**

Ce sont is used in describing two or more things or to introduce several people.

>**Ici, ce sont les toilettes.**
>**Ce sont Nathalie et Frédéric.**

 § 3   **The Verb** *avoir*

Avoir (*to have*) is an irregular verb.

>**J'ai faim.**   *I am hungry.*
>**Tu as soif.**   *You are thirsty.*
>**Il a vingt ans.**   *He is twenty years old.*

avoir

j'	ai
tu	as
il /elle /on	a
nous	avons
vous	avez
ils /elles	ont

Note the pronunciation of **ils ont / elles ont**: Liaison occurs between the pronouns and the verb. That is, the **s** is pronounced and carried over to the following vowel.

The expression **il y a** contains the verb **avoir. Il y a** can mean *there is* or *there are*. For example, you can use **il y a** if you want to express who or what is located in a certain place. The appropriate place designations can come at the beginning of the sentence (separated by a comma), or at the end.

>**Sur le marché, il y a des oranges. / Il y a des oranges sur le marché.**

§ 4   **1st-Group Verbs**

Most French verbs fall into this group. These are regular verbs whose infinitive ends in **-er.**

adorer *(to love, adore)*

j'	ador**e**
tu	ador**es**
il /elle /on	ador**e**
nous	ador**ons**
vous	ador**ez**
ils /elles	ador**ent**

With **-er** verbs the three singular persons and the third person plural sound alike because the endings of these forms are not heard in speech. Only the endings **-ons** and **-ez** are pronounced.

Pay attention to the liaison when the verb begins with a vowel or a mute **h**; also note that **je** is shortened to **j'.**
In this group there are some verbs that have regular endings but peculiarities in their stem.

Verbs Ending in *-ger* and *-cer*

With the verb **manger** (*to eat*) and other verbs ending in **-ger**, there is a peculiarity in the first person plural: To keep the pronunciation the same as with the other forms, an **-e-** is inserted:
je mange – nous mangeons

manger

je	mange
tu	manges
il /elle /on	mange
nous	man**geons**
vous	mangez
ils /elles	mangent

The verb **commencer** (*to begin*) and other verbs ending in **-cer** are handled in a similar way. Here the **c** is written with a cédille (**ç**) to produce a soft **s** in the spoken language:
je commence – nous commençons

commencer

je	commence
tu	commences
il/elle/on	commence
nous	commençons
vous	commencez
ils/elles	commencent

Stem-Changing Verbs

Verbs Ending in -eter and -éter

Acheter *(to buy)* is one of the **-er** verbs. The peculiarity of this verb is that the three singular persons and the third person plural have accentuated stem forms, so they have an accent: **j'achète**, **tu achètes**, **il achète**, and **ils achètent**. The first and second persons plural are stressed on the ending, so they retain the infinitive stem **achet-** and are written without an accent: **nous achetons**, **vous achetez**.

acheter

j'	achète
tu	achètes
il/elle/on	achète
nous	achetons
vous	achetez
ils/elles	achètent

The verb **préférer** *(to prefer)* is conjugated like **acheter**. In the stem-accentuated forms (that is, the three singular persons and the third person plural), the second **é** changes to **è** (**je préfère**). The first and second persons plural, which are stressed on the endings, retain the infinitive stem **préfér-** and are written with two *accents aigus*: **nous préférons**, **vous préférez**.

préférer

je	préfère
tu	préfères
il/elle/on	préfère
nous	préférons
vous	préférez
ils/elles	préfèrent

Verbs Ending in -eler

With the verbs **appeler** *(to call)* and **s'appeler** *(to be named)*, as well as with other verbs ending in **-eler**, the forms of the three singular persons and the third person plural are stressed on the stem. These forms therefore double the **l**: **j'appelle**, **tu appelles**, **il appelle**, **ils appellent**. The forms that are stressed on the ending have just one **l**; that is, they retain the infinitive stem **appel-**: **nous appelons**, **vous appelez**.

appeler

j'	appelle
tu	appelles
il/elle/on	appelle
nous	appelons
vous	appelez
ils/elles	appellent

S'appeler is a reflexive verb.
▶ § 25 Reflexive Verbs

§ 5   2nd-Group Verbs

This group includes the verbs that end in **-ir**: **finir** *(to finish)*
The verbs of this group have the stem expansion using **-iss-** in the three plural persons (**nous finissons**, **vous finissez**, **ils finissent**).

finir

je	finis
tu	finis
il/elle/on	finit
nous	finissons
vous	finissez
ils/elles	finissent

§ 6   3rd-Group Verbs

This group includes all other verbs that are partially or completely irregular: **prendre** (*to take*).

Verbs Ending in *-tir*

The 3rd group also includes some verbs that end in **-ir** and don't exhibit the **-iss-** stem expansion, such as the verbs ending in **-tir**: **partir** (*to leave*), **sortir** (*to go out*).

partir		sortir	
je	pars	je	sors
tu	pars	tu	sors
il/elle/on	part	il/elle/on	sort
nous	partons	nous	sortons
vous	partez	vous	sortez
ils/elles	partent	ils/elles	sortent

Verbs Ending in *-mir*

The 3rd group also includes a few **-ir** verbs that don't exhibit the **-iss-** stem expansion, such as verbs ending in **-mir**: **dormir** (*to sleep*).

dormir

je	dors
tu	dors
il/elle/on	dort
nous	dormons
vous	dormez
ils/elles	dorment

Verbs Ending in *-ire*

Verbs in **-ire** belong to the 3rd group. They include such verbs as **construire** (*to construct, build*), **produire** (*to produce*), and **conduire** (*to drive*).

construire

je	construis
tu	construis
il/elle/on	construit
nous	construisons
vous	construisez
ils/elles	construisent

 § 7   The Verb *aller*

Aller (*to go*) ends in **-er**, but it is irregular. Only the first and second persons plural retain the infinitive stem **all-** in forming the present-tense forms (**nous allons**, **vous allez**).

aller

je	vais
tu	vas
il/elle/on	va
nous	allons
vous	allez
ils/elles	vont

Several prepositions can be used after **aller**:

– **en** and **à** with places:
  On va en France.
  Tu vas à Paris ?
– **en** and **à** with means of transportation:
  On va en train à Bruxelles.
  Elle va à vélo en ville.
– **chez** with persons:
  Fred et Nathalie vont chez Jean-Guy et Laure.

 § 8   The Verb *s'asseoir*

The verb **s'asseoir** has two conjugations: The forms of the first conjugation are formed with **-ie-** or **-ey-**; the forms of the second conjugation are formed using **-oi-** or **-oy-**. Normally a mixture of the two conjugations is used. The most commonly used forms are in bold type (you don't even need to learn the other forms):

je m'	assieds	**je m'**	**assois**
tu t'	assieds	**tu t'**	**assois**
il/elle/on s'	assied	**il/elle/on s'**	**assoit**
nous nous	**asseyons**	nous nous	assoyons
vous vous	**asseyez**	vous vous	assoyez
ils s'	asseyent	**ils/elles s'**	**assoient**

§9 The Verb *boire*

The verb **boire** is irregular. The first and second persons plural form the present tense using the stem **buv-** (**nous buvons, vous buvez**).

boire

je	bois
tu	bois
il/elle/on	boit
nous	buvons
vous	buvez
ils/elles	boivent

 §10 The Verb *connaître*

Connaître *(to know)* is an irregular verb of the third verb group.
Note the stem expansion using **-aiss-** in the three plural forms and the *accent circonflexe* in the third person singular (**il connaît**).

connaître

je	connais
tu	connais
il/elle/on	connaît
nous	connaissons
vous	connaissez
ils/elles	connaissent

 §11 The Verb *croire*

The verb **croire** *(to believe)* is irregular. Note the first and second persons plural, which form the present tense using **y** (**nous croyons, vous croyez**).

croire

je	crois
tu	crois
il/elle/on	croit
nous	croyons
vous	croyez
ils/elles	croient

The conjunction **que** can be used after the verb **croire: Je crois que c'est vrai.**

§12 The Verb *dire*

The verb **dire** *(to say)* is irregular.
The second person plural of **dire, vous dites,** has a form similar to the second person of **être, vous êtes,** and of **faire, vous faites.**

dire

je	dis
tu	dis
il/elle/on	dit
nous	disons
vous	dites
ils/elles	disent

Dire is used with the preposition **à: dire quelque chose à quelqu'un.** Don't forget: **à** followed by the definite article **le** or **les** changes to **au** or **aux**, respectively.

§13 The Verb *faire*

Faire *(to make, to do)* is an irregular verb.

faire

je	fais
tu	fais
il/elle/on	fait
nous	faisons
vous	faites
ils/elles	font

Note the pronunciation of the first person plural: **nous faisons: ai** is pronounced like a mute **e**.

§ 14 **The Verb** *pouvoir*

Pouvoir *(can, may, to be able)* is a modal verb. It is irregular; only the first and second persons plural retain the infinitive stem **pouv-** in forming the present tense (**nous pouvons**, **vous pouvez**).
▸ § 24 The Modal Verbs

pouvoir

je	peux
tu	peux
il/elle/on	peut
nous	pouvons
vous	pouvez
ils/elles	peuvent

 § 15 **The Verb** *prendre*

The verb **prendre** is irregular. Note the nasal sound in the three singular forms. The third person plural, in contrast, has no nasal sound and is pronounced with an open **e** (**ils prennent**). The first and second persons plural are distinguished by a mute **e**.
The verbs **comprendre** and **apprendre** are conjugated with the same pattern.

prendre

je	prends
tu	prends
il/elle/on	prend
nous	prenons
vous	prenez
ils/elles	prennent

 § 16 **The Verb** *savoir*

The verb **savoir** is irregular. The three plural forms retain the infinitive stem **sav-** in forming the present tense (**nous savons**, **vous savez**, **ils savent**).

savoir

je	sais
tu	sais
il/elle/on	sait
nous	savons
vous	savez
ils/elles	savent

 § 17 **The Verb** *venir*

The verb **venir** *(to come)* is irregular: Only the first and second persons plural are formed on the basis of the infinitive stem (**nous venons**, **vous venez**).

venir

je	viens
tu	viens
il/elle/on	vient
nous	venons
vous	venez
ils/elles	viennent

 § 18 **The Verb** *voir*

The verb **voir** *(to see)* is irregular. Note the first and second persons plural, which contruct the present forms with **y** (**nous voyons**, **vous voyez**).

voir

je	vois
tu	vois
il/elle/on	voit
nous	voyons
vous	voyez
ils/elles	voient

§19 The Verb *vouloir*

Vouloir *(to want)* is a modal verb. It is irregular. Only the first and second persons plural retain the infinitive stem **voul-** in forming the present tense (**nous voulons, vous voulez**).
▶ § 24 The Modal Verbs

vouloir

je	veux
tu	veux
il/elle/on	veut
nous	voulons
vous	voulez
ils/elles	veulent

When you want to order something, it is more polite to say **Je voudrais** rather than **Je veux**. **Je voudrais** is the conditional form of **vouloir**.

§20 The Past

The Passé composé

The passé composé expresses action in past time. It consists of two elements: the present-tense form of the helping verb (**avoir** or **être**) + the past participle (**participe passé**) of the appropriate verb.
▶ § 22 The Past Participle

– The Passé composé with *avoir*

The passé composé with **avoir** consists of the present-tense form of **avoir** and the past participle of the appropriate verb.
Nous avons mangé des frites.

In a negative sentence, the negating elements surround the conjugated form of **avoir**:
Nous n'avons pas mangé de frites.

The verbs **avoir** and **être** form the passé composé with **avoir**.

avoir	j'ai eu	*I had, have had, did have*
être	j'ai été	*I was, have been*

– The Passé composé with *être*

The passé composé with **être** consists of the present-tense form of **être** and the past participle of the appropriate verb.
Jean-Guy est allé au concert.

Only a few verbs form the passé composé with **être**; these include the verbs of motion: **aller, venir, arriver, partir, entrer, sortir, rentrer, monter, descendre, revenir,** und **rester**.

In forming the passé composé with **être**, the past participle agrees in gender and number with the subject of the sentence.
Laure est allée au concert.
Frédéric et Nathalie ne sont pas allés au concert.
Nous sommes arrivées ce soir. (Laure et Nathalie)

In a negative sentence **ne** and **pas** surround the conjugated form of **être**:
Nathalie n'est pas allée au concert.

§21 The Immediate Past

The expression **venir de faire quelque chose** expresses the immediate past. The conjugated form of **venir** is followed by **de** and a verb in the infinitive form.
Je viens d'arriver. *I have just arrived.*
Je viens de la voir. *I have just seen her.*

Careful! This expression must not be confused with **venir de** + location:
Je viens de Paris. *I come from Paris.*

§ 22   The Past Participle

The past participle (**participe passé**) is used in forming the passé composé, among other things.

1st-Group Verbs:

These form their past participle by ending in **-é**:
demander   ▷ **demandé**

2nd-Group Verbs:

These form their past participle by ending in **-i**:
finir   ▷ **fini**

3rd-Group Verbs:

être	**été**	J'ai été en Allemagne.
avoir	**eu**	Tu as eu faim.
aller	allé	Elle est allée à Paris.
faire	fait	Jean-Guy a fait la vaisselle.
prendre	pris	J'ai pris le train.
dire	dit	Elle a dit bonjour.
s'asseoir	assis	Ils se sont assis sur la terrasse.
partir	parti	Ils sont partis ce matin.
dormir	dormi	Nous avons bien dormi.
produire	produit	Qu'est-ce qu'ils ont produit ?
voir	vu	Avez-vous vu Nathalie ?
connaître	connu	Nous avons bien connu Jean.
pouvoir	pu	J'ai pu dormir un peu.
venir	venu	Il est venu en train.
boire	bu	Tu as bu une bonne bière.
savoir	su	Elle a su trouver le café.
vouloir	voulu	J'ai voulu dire quelque chose.
croire	cru	Tu as cru à cette histoire ?

 § 23   The Future Tense

The Futur proche
The futur proche is used for events in the near future that also have a connection to the present.
This tense is often used to express a preference or an opinion.

The futur proche consists of two elements: the present-tense form of **aller** + the infinitive of the verb:

near future	aller	infinitive	
Ce soir,	je vais	manger	une pizza.
Demain,	tu vas	visiter	le Louvre ?
Dimanche,	on va	partir	en Belgique.

 § 24   Modal Verbs

The modal verbs (**pouvoir**, **vouloir**) are followed by an infinitive.
▷ § 14 The verb **pouvoir**
▷ § 19 The verb **vouloir**

> **On peut aller à la mer.**
> *We can go to the sea.*
> **Elles veulent partir à midi.**
> *They want to leave at noon.*

With negative sentences the **ne** comes right after the subject pronoun; **pas** (or **jamais**, etc.) comes after the modal verb and before the infinitive:
Il ne veut pas conduire.

 § 25   Reflexive Verbs

With reflexive verbs, the pronouns refer back to the subject. They come before the verb.

Singular		Plural	
me	*myself*	**nous**	*ourselves*
te	*yourself*	**vous**	*yourself / yourselves (polite and / or plural)*
se	*himself, herself, oneself*	**se**	*themselves*

Before vowels **me**, **te**, **se**, change to **m'**, **t'**, **s'**.
The verb is conjugated in accordance with its group—in this instance, **s'amuser** (*to have fun*):

s'amuser
je m'	amuse
tu t'	amuses
il/elle/on s'	amuse

nous nous   amusons
vous vous   amusez
ils/elles s'   amusent

In negative sentences, **ne** comes right after the subject pronoun; **pas** (or **jamais**, etc.) comes after the verb: **Ils ne s'amusent pas.**

 § 26   **Impersonal Expressions**

il faut + infinitive

When an infinitive follows **il faut**, it expresses obligation. The negative means that the action is not permitted or not required.

In most cases the negative form of **il faut** is the equivalent of a command, so it means that something is not permitted: **Il ne faut pas fumer** means *It is forbidden to smoke* or *No smoking* (rather than *It is not necessary to smoke*).

Il faut visiter le vieux port.
You have to visit the old port.
Il ne faut pas manger sur la plage.
Eating on the beach is not permitted./ One must not eat on the beach.

il faut + noun

When **il faut** is followed by a noun, it means that the specified item is needed.

Pour une tarte aux pommes, il faut du beurre.
You need butter to make an apple pie.

 § 27   **Pronouns**

1. Subject Pronouns

The subject pronouns are:

Singular
1st Person   **je**   *I*
2nd Person   **tu**   *you*

3rd Person	**il**	*he*
	elle	*she*
	on	*one/we*

Plural
1st Person   **nous**   *we*
2nd Person   **vous**   *you*
3rd Person   **ils**   *they (masculine)*
             elles   *they (feminine)*

Before a vowel or a mute **h**, **je** changes to **j'**. There is no separate word that translates *it*.
On can be used to construct impersonal or passive-voice sentences:
   On parle anglais.
   English is spoken.

In the spoken language **on** is frequently used in the sense of *we*: **On est d'ici.** (*We are from here.*)

Ils refers to a group that is either all masculine or a mixture of masculine and feminine people or things.
   Ils = Frédéric + Nathalie or
       Frédéric + Jean-Guy

Elles refers exclusively to a group of feminine people or items:
   Elles = Nathalie + Laure.

2. Direct Object Pronouns

Direct object pronouns generally take the place of nouns.

me	nous
te	vous
le/la	les

Before a vowel, **me** is shortened to **m'**, **te** to **t'**, and **le** and **la** to **l'**.

Le stands for a masculine singular noun.
La stands for a feminine singular noun.
Les stands for a masculine and/or feminine plural noun.

Object pronouns come before the verb to which they belong.
Ne and **pas** surround the object pronouns and the verb.

Tu m'aimes ?	– **Oui, je t'aime.**
Vous prenez le bus ?	– **Oui, je le prends.**
	– **Non, je ne le prends pas.**

With verbs that are followed by an infinitive, the object pronouns come before the infinitive.
– **Tu vas chercher Nathalie et Frédéric ?**
– **Oui, je vais les chercher.**
– **Non, je ne vais pas les chercher.**

Object pronouns are also used in sentences without a verb, for example, with **voilà**:
Le voilà !
Te voilà !

3. Indirect Object Pronouns

Indirect object pronouns stand for persons and have the same forms in the first and second persons singular and plural as the direct object pronouns: **me**, **te**, **nous**, **vous**.
In the third person singular and plural, the indirect object pronouns are **lui** and **leur**, respectively. **Lui** stands for either a male or a female person.
Leur stands for several male and/or several female people.

Je te téléphone.
Je téléphone à un cousin. Je lui téléphone.
Je téléphone à des collègues. Je leur téléphone.

The preposition **à** follows the verbs **demander**, **donner**, **manquer**, **téléphoner**, etc.
Je demande à Paul ...

These verbs require indirect object pronouns.
Je lui demande ...

The indirect object pronouns are used in the same place in the sentence as the direct object pronouns.

The placement of the elements of negation **ne** and **pas** is the same as with the direct object pronouns.
Je ne lui téléphone pas.

4. The Accentuating Personal Pronouns

In French, in addition to the nonaccentuating personal pronouns (**je**, **tu**, **il / elle / on**, **nous**, **vous**, **ils / elles**), there are accentuating (disjunctive) personal pronouns.

moi	nous
toi	vous
lui /elle	eux /elles

The accentuating personal pronouns are used:
– to introduce oneself or another person:
  Moi, c'est Nathalie.
– in shortened sentences with no verb:
  Et toi, Laure, tu es professeur ?
– after prepositions and conjunctions:
  Tu manges avec moi ?
– for emphasis and with contrasts:
  Moi, je fais les courses.
– to express one's opinion in expressions such as:
  • answers to affirmative sentences:
    accentuating personal pronoun + **aussi** (also)
    accentuating personal pronoun + **non / pas** (not)
    J'adore les moules. – Moi aussi. / Moi pas.
    I love mussels. Me too. / Not me.
    The form **pas moi** is colloquial.
  • Answers to negative sentences:
    accentuating personal pronouns + **non plus** (also not)
    accentuating personal pronouns + **si** (yes [on the contrary])
    Je ne mange pas de fromage. – Moi non plus. / Moi si.
    I don't eat cheese.—Neither do I. I do.

5. The Pronoun *y*

The pronoun **y** stands for places that are introduced by **à**, **en**, **dans**, **sur**, or **sous**. The English equivalent is *there*.

> **Frédéric travaille à l'aéroport. Il y travaille.**
> **Il va en Italie. Il y va.**

The pronoun **y** is subject to the same rules of placement as for the object pronouns: **y** always comes before the verb:

> **Il y va souvent.**   before the conjugated verb
> **Il va y habiter.**   before the infinitve to
>   which it refers

The elements of negation surround the pronoun and the conjugated verb:

> **Il n'y est pas allé depuis Noël.**

 § 28   Noun Gender

The ending of a noun often indicates its gender. With a few exceptions, words with the following endings are feminine:

-ée	la soirée, la journée
-té	la spécialité, la santé
-tion	la situation, la destination
-ette	la baguette, la casquette
-ade	la salade, la balade
-ie	la charcuterie, la crêperie
-ise	la chemise, la cerise
-logie	l'astrologie

Further feminine nouns:

brands of automobiles	**une Mercedes, une Renault**

With a few exceptions, nouns with these endings are masculine:

-ment	le moment, l'instrument
-age	le garage, le fromage
-eau	le bureau, le gâteau
-in	le vin, le jardin
-isme	le tourisme
-ail	le travail
-phone	le téléphone

Further masculine nouns:

languages	**le français, le hollandais ...**
the days of the week	**le lundi, le mardi ...**
the colors	**le bleu, le rouge ...**

Names of Countries

Country names are generally used with the definite article. In French there are masculine and feminine country names.

feminine
la France	**l'Allemagne**

masculine
le Maroc	**les Etats-Unis** *(m./Pl.)*

Professional Titles

Sometimes these nouns have only one form for both sexes because they designate professions that formerly were practiced mostly by men. If they refer to a woman, the female gender will be made clear by context. If the context is not clear enough, the word **femme** (*woman*) can be inserted:

> **un médecin / une femme médecin**

With national diplomats, **Madame** is placed before the professional designation:

> **l'ambassadeur / Madame l'ambassadeur**

With some of these professional titles, the gender is indicated only through the article; the spelling and pronunciation are the same:

> **le journaliste / la journaliste**
> **le ministre / la ministre**

If the noun begins with a vowel, the gender must be deduced from context:

> **l'architecte**

Some professional designations do have a masculine and a feminine form:

> **le vendeur / la vendeuse**

§29 Formation of Plural Nouns

In French the plural of a noun is generally indicated with a silent **-s**:

le chocolat	**les chocolats**
la maison	**les maisons**

If a noun already ends in an **-s**, it doesn't change in the plural:

le pastis	**les pastis**

Some nouns have an irregular plural, such as the nouns that end in **-eau**. They form their plural in **-x**, which is silent.

le gâteau	**les gâteaux**

If a noun already ends in **-x** in the singular, it doesn't change in the plural.

le prix	**les prix**

Nouns ending in **-al** and **-ail** form their plural in **-aux**.

le journal	**les journaux**
le travail	**les travaux**

There are a couple of special cases:

monsieur	▶	**messieurs**
madame	▶	**mesdames**
mademoiselle	▶	**mesdemoiselles**

 §30 Asking Questions

Intonation Questions

Intonation (the melody of a sentence) can change a declarative sentence into a question.

Il est d'ici.
Il est d'ici ?

In the spoken language the intonation question is the most common format.

Questions with *est-ce que*

In posing a question with **est-ce que**, this expression is placed before a declarative sentence. The word order is the same as with the declarative sentence, as is the melody of the sentence. Before a vowel **est-ce que** contracts to **est-ce qu'**.

Est-ce que Jean-Guy est d'ici ?
Est-ce qu'il est d'ici ?

The interrogative form with **est-ce que** can be used in both the written and the spoken language.

Inversion Questions

A declarative sentence also can be made into a question by reversing the order of subject and verb (inversion). When the subject is a pronoun, the subject pronoun is connected to the verb with a hyphen.

Il est pilote. ▶ **Est-il pilote ?**

A **t** is inserted between the verb and the subject pronoun in the third person singular to facilitate pronunciation when the verb form ends in **-e** or **-a**.

Elle mange bien.	**Mange-t-elle bien ?**
Il a faim.	**A-t-il faim ?**

If the subject is not a pronoun, but rather a noun (for example, a person's name), it is repeated after the verb with the corresponding subject pronoun:

Marc est-il à la maison ?

Inversion questions are characteristic of a fairly elevated language level and are used primarily in writing.

Yes-or-No Questions

These are questions that can be answered with **oui** or **non**.

Tu es d'ici ? – Non, je suis de Cauteret.
On mange ? – Oui, bien sûr !

§31 Demonstrative Adjectives

Demonstrative adjectives always come before the noun to which they refer. In the singular there are two masculine and two feminine forms; in the plural, though, there is just one form: **ces** for masculine or feminine nouns.

ce magasin	*this store* before masculine singular nouns beginning with a consonant
cet apéritif	*this aperitif* before masculine singular nouns beginning with a vowel or a mute **h**
cette dame	*this lady* before feminine singular nouns
ces magasins	*these stores*
ces apéritifs	*these aperitifs*
ces dames	*these ladies* before masculine or feminine plural nouns

§32 Question Words

Questions that can't be answered with **oui** or **non** require a more complete answer. They are always constructed with a question word.
The question word can come at the beginning or the end of an intonation question:

Où est le restaurant ?
Le restaurant est où ?
Where is the restaurant?

Such questions can also be constructed with **est-ce que**. The question word is placed at the beginning of the sentence, followed by **est-ce que** or **est-ce qu'** and the rest of the words in declarative sentence order.

Qu'est-ce que vous aimez ?
What do you like?

The Question Word *quel*

The question word **quel** agrees in gender and number with the noun to which it refers.
In English the basic meaning is *which* or *what*.

Quel sandwich est-ce que vous prenez ?
Which sandwich . . .?
Quelle profession est-ce que vous avez ?
What is your profession?
Quels gâteaux est-ce que vous aimez ?
Which cakes do you like?
Quelles tomates est-ce que vous voulez ?
Which tomatoes . . .?

Quel is also used in conjuction with **heure**:
à quelle heure means *at what time*.
Quel can also be used to express enthusiasm:
Quelle jolie maison !

In this case **quel / quelle** means *what a*.

The Question Word *qui*

The question word **qui** means *who* or *whom*.
   Qui est-ce ?   *Who is it?*

It is invariable and can also be used in combination with prepositions:

pour qui	*for whom*
à qui	*to whom*
de qui	*from whom*
avec qui	*with whom*

Further Question Words

que / qu'	*what*
quoi	*what*
où	*where*
d'où	*from where*
comment	*how*
pourquoi	*why*
quand	*when*
combien	*how much, how many*
combien de temps	*how long*

▼

With intonation questions where the question word comes at the end, **que** changes to **quoi**. Both mean *what*.

Qu'est-ce que vous mangez ?
Vous mangez quoi ?
What are you eating?

 §33 **Negation**

ne ... pas
In French, negation essentially consists of two elements: **ne** and **pas**. **Ne** comes before the verb, and **pas** after it. Before a vowel or a mute **h**, **ne** contracts to **n'**.

Je ne suis pas pilote.
Nathalie et Frédéric ne sont pas de Nice.

In casual conversation, after **je**, **tu**, **nous**, **vous** and before consonants, **ne** is frequently pronounced as **n** or left out entirely. **Je ne peux pas** thus becomes **Je n'peux pas. / Je peux pas.**

ne ... pas de
The negation **ne . . . pas de** expresses the quantity *zero*; the English equivalent is *not any*.
Vous n'avez pas de pommes ?
Sur le marché, il n'y a pas de tomates italiennes.

Il n'y a pas de ... means *there is / are no . . .*

ne ... plus, ne ... rien, ne ... jamais
These negations also surround the verb in the same way as **ne ... pas.**

Il ne mange plus.
He is not eating any more.
Il ne va jamais au concert.
He never goes to the concert.
Elle ne prend rien comme dessert.
She has nothing for dessert.

The quantity *zero* is expressed in French with **ne . . . pas de**. The following negations also express the quantity zero:

Il n'y a plus d'oranges.
There are no more oranges.
Elle ne boit jamais d'alcool.
She never drinks alcohol.
Il n'y a rien de nouveau.
There is nothing new.

ne ... ni ... ni
The negation **ne . . . ni . . . ni** means *neither . . . nor*. **Ni** is repeated before every verb or noun in the enumeration. It is used without an article:

Il ne peut ni manger ni boire.
Il ne mange ni artichaut ni tomate ni endive.

 §34 **Adjectives**

Adjective Forms

Adjectives agree in gender and number with the nouns to which they refer, so they may exist in four forms:

	masculine	feminine
Singular	grand	grande
Plural	grands	grandes

With adjectives that end in a vowel, the pronunciation remains the same:

	masculine	feminine
Singular	vrai	vraie
Plural	vrais	vraies

Adjectives that already end in **-e** in the masculine form have no separate feminine form, and there is no difference in pronunciation:
masculine and feminine singular: **jeune**
masculine and feminine plural: **jeunes**

If the adjective refers to several nouns of different gender, the masculine plural form is used:

Jean-Guy, Laure et Nathalie ne sont pas très grands.

In the plural the indefinite article is shortened from **des** to **de** when an adjective precedes the noun:

Ils ont des maisons.
Ils ont de grandes maisons.

Adjective Position

As in English, adjectives can be connected to nouns by a verb (usually **être**).

Le musée est intéressant.

In French the adjectives normally come after the noun.

C'est un musée intéressant.

In some cases adjectives come before the nouns.

C'est un petit musée.

Adjectives that come before the nouns they modify include:

grand/e	joli/e
petit/e	bon/bonne
gros/grosse	mauvais/e
jeune	court/e

Sometimes the meaning also changes depending on whether the adjective comes before or after the noun.

Special Considerations

cher

Some adjectives have irregular forms; one example is the adjective **cher**.

Le café est cher.
La bière est chère.
Les cafés sont chers.
Les bières sont chères.

The pronunciation of these four forms is the same.

vieux, beau, nouveau

The adjective **vieux** (*old*)—like two other important adjectives, **beau** (*beautiful, handsome*) and **nouveau** (*new*)—has two masculine singular forms:

vieux / beau / nouveau
before nouns that begin with a consonant

vieil / bel / nouvel
before nouns that begin with a vowel or a mute **h**

un vieux vélo, un vieil hôtel, une vieille voiture, de vieux hôtels, de vieilles voitures

bon

The adjective **bon** has a special feminine form: **bonne**.

	masculine	feminine
Singular	bon	bonne
Plural	bons	bonnes

Note the pronunciation of the adjective before a vowel: **bon** + a noun that begins with a vowel is pronounced the same way as **bonne**, and the **n** is carried over to the following vowel.

une bonne bière
un bon artichaut

Adjectives of Nationality

Adjectives of nationality, like most adjectives, take an **-e** in the feminine form and an **-s** in the plural:

	masculine	feminine
Singular	américain	américaine
Plural	américains	américaines

If the adjective ends in an **-s** in the masculine singular, it remains the same in the masculine plural:

	masculine	feminine
Singular	français	française
Plural	français	françaises

With adjectives of nationality that have a nasal sound in the masculine form (**-ain**), the feminine form is pronounced without the nasal sound, for the added **e** affects the division into syllables: **américain, américaine.**

With adjectives of nationality that end in **-ien** in the masculine form, **-ne** is added to the feminine form, and it is not pronounced with a nasal sound: **italien / italienne**.

With adjectives of nationality that end in **-e**, the masculine and feminine forms sound the same, for example, **belge / belge**, **corse / corse**.

The designation of nationality is written with a capital letter.

    Il est Français.   *He is a Frenchman.*

Adjectives of Color

Adjectives of color behave like other adjectives: They agree in gender and number with the nouns to which they refer. Adjectives of color come after the noun.

With adjectives of color that end in **-e** in the masculine form, the feminine form remains the same (**rouge**, **jaune**): **un pantalon rouge**, **une robe rouge**.

Marron and **orange** are invariable:
    un pantalon orange, des pantalons orange

 § 35   **Adverbs**

The Adverb *bien*

The adjective **bon / bonne** (*good*) and its corresponding adverb **bien** are used very frequently in the spoken language. Thus it is important to be able to distinguish this special form of the adverb from the adjective.

C'est bon stands for sense perceptions; **c'est bien** is used when something is being evaluated.
    Le champagne, c'est bon ?
    Aller à vélo, c'est écologique, c'est bien !

In most cases adverbs clarify verbs.
    Monsieur Leclerc conduit bien.
    Mr. Leclerc drives well.

 § 36   **Prepositions**

The Preposition *à*

à and the Definite Article

If the definite article **le** or **les** follows the preposition **à**, the two combine.

    à + le = **au**
    à + les = **aux**

But: à + la = **à la**
       à + l'   = **à l'**

    On va au cinéma ?
    Vous allez aux Etats-Unis ?

But: **Tu vas à la cantine ?**
       Je vais à l'aéroport.

à After Certain Verbs

The preposition **à** is also used in conjunction with certain verbs, such as **demander, donner, téléphoner**, etc.:
    Je demande à la dame.
    Je téléphone à Julie.

The Preposition *de*

de and the Definite Article

De means *from* (**Je suis de Cauteret.**) or *of* (**le cousin de Frédéric**).
Before a vowel or a mute **h**, **de** contracts to **d'**. (**Tu viens d'où ?**)

If the preposition **de** is followed by the definite article **le** or **les**, the two of them combine.

    de + le   = **du**
    de + les = **des**

But: de + la = **de la**
       de + l'   = **de l'**

    Tu es du Maroc.
    Nous sommes des Etats-Unis.

But: **Je suis de La Rochelle.**
       Elle vient de l'île de Ré.

▼

de After Expressions of Quantity

un kilo de/d' ...   *a kilo of . . .*

No article is used after expressions of quantity + **de / d'.**

   Une bouteille de pastis.

Prepositions: Countries and Cities

There are some special considerations when specifying a city or a country as a destination (to where?), a residence (where?), or place of origin (from where?):

Cities:
à means *in* and *to*; **de** means *from*:

   J'habite à Strasbourg.
   Je vais à Nice.
   Je suis de Paris.

With city names such as **Le Caire** and **Le Havre**, the combination involving the preposition **à** takes place:

   Je vais au Caire.
   Je suis du Havre.

City names in combination with **habiter** needn't use the preposition **à**: **J'habite Strasbourg.**

Countries:
En and **à** mean *in* and *to*; **de** means *from*:

l'Australie	▶ **en Australie/d'Australie**
le Maroc à	▶ **au Maroc/du Maroc**
les Etats-Unis	▶ **aux Etats-Unis/ des Etats-Unis**

With feminine country names, **en** and **de** are used without an article: **en France/de France.** With masculine country names, **à** is used with an article = **au/du: au Portugal/du Portugal.** With plural country names, **à** and **de** are used with the article in the plural = **aux/des: aux Etats-Unis/des Etats-Unis.**

With masculine country names that begin with a vowel, **en** and **de** are used without an article: **en Israël/d'Israël.**

Prepositions: Means of Transportation

Two different prepositions are used with means of transportation: **à** and **en.**

If you sit on the means of transportation, **à** is used: **à vélo, à moto.**

If you sit in the means of transportation, **en** is used: **en voiture, en métro, en bus, en train, en avion.**

Other Prepositions

Sans means *without* and is used without an article (**Un café sans sucre**). Sometimes English uses the word *-free* for French expressions using **sans** (**de l'essence sans plomb** = *lead-free gasoline*).

Prepositions of Place:

à côté de	*beside, next to*
à gauche de	*to the left of*
à droite de	*to the right of*
en face de	*facing, across from*
au milieu de	*in the middle of*
après	*after*
dans	*in*
derrière	*behind*
devant	*in front of*
près de	*near*
sur	*on*
sous	*under*
vers	*toward*

Note that the preposition **de** in **à côté de, à gauche de**, etc., is used with the definite articles **du, de la, ,de l', des: C'est à côté du café.**

Prepositions of Time:

à	*at*
après	*after*
avant	*before*
dans	*in*
en	*in*
jusque	*until*
pendant	*during*
pour	*for (duration)*

§ 37   Cardinal Numbers

The Cardinal Numbers From 0 Through 10

0 **zéro**	6 **six**
1 **un**	7 **sept**
2 **deux**	8 **huit**
3 **trois**	9 **neuf**
4 **quatre**	10 **dix**
5 **cinq**	

Six and **dix** have an unvoiced **x**.

The pronunciation of some of these numbers changes as soon as the numbers are accompanied by a determiner, rather than standing alone.

Cardinal Numbers From 11 Through 100

11 onze	18 dix-huit
12 douze	19 dix-neuf
13 treize	20 vingt
14 quatorze	21 vingt et un
15 quinze	22 vingt-deux
16 seize	23 vingt-trois
17 dix-sept	

...
The numbers from 17 on consist of a ten + a hyphen + a unit:
dix-sept, **vingt-neuf** ... all the way to 69.
32 trente-deux
33 trente-trois
34 trente-quatre
35 trente-cinq

...
20, 30, 40, 50, and 60 are:
20 vingt
30 trente
40 quarante
50 cinquante
60 soixante

With 21, 31, 41, 51, 61, the 1 is connected using the word **et** without a hyphen:

21	vingt et un
31	trente et un
41	quarante et un
51	cinquante et un
61	soixante et un

From 70 through 79, "addition" takes place (e.g., **soixante-dix** = 60 + 10); 80 is formed through multiplication (**quatre-vingts** = 4 x 20); then multiplication and addition are used (e.g., 90, **quatre-vingt-dix** = 4 x 20 + 10)!

70 soixante-dix	85 quatre-vingt-cinq
71 soixante et onze	86 quatre-vingt-six
72 soixante-douze	87 quatre-vingt-sept
73 soixante-treize	88 quatre-vingt-huit
74 soixante-quatorze	89 quatre-vingt-neuf
75 soixante-quinze	90 quatre-vingt-dix
76 soixante-seize	91 quatre-vingt-onze
77 soixante-dix-sept	92 quatre-vingt-douze
78 soixante-dix-huit	93 quatre-vingt-treize
79 soixante-dix-neuf	94 quatre-vingt-quatorze
80 quatre-vingts	95 quatre-vingt-quinze
81 quatre-vingt-un	96 quatre-vingt-seize
82 quatre-vingt-deux	97 quatre-vingt-dix-sept
83 quatre-vingt-trois	98 quatre-vingt-dix-huit
84 quatre-vingt-quatre	99 quatre-vingt-dix-neuf

100 is **cent**.

Cardinal Numbers Above 100

101 cent un	1000 mille
102 cent deux	1001 mille un
180 cent quatre-vingts	2000 deux mille
200 deux cents	
201 deux cent un	
281 deux cent quatre-vingts	

§ 38   Ordinal Numbers

The ordinal numbers are formed by adding the ending **-ième** to the cardinal numbers. With cardinal numbers that end in **-e**, the **-e** is removed before the **-ième** ending. The ordinal numbers are usually written in abbreviated form.

1er le premier
1ère la première
2e le / la deuxième
    le second, la seconde
3e le / la troisième
10e le / la dixième

20e le / la vingtième
21e le / la vingt et unième
30e le / la trentième
70e le / la soixante-dixième
71e le / la soixante et onzième
80e le / la quatre-vingtième
81e le / la quatre-vingt-unième
94e le / la quatre-vingt-quartorzième
99e le / la quatre-vingt-dix-neuvième
100e le / la centième
1000e le / la millième

- Only with **premier** and **second** is there a separate feminine form: **la première**, **la seconde**. Otherwise, the masculine and feminine forms are identical: e.g., **le dixième**, **la dixième**.
- The article is never contracted before a vowel or a mute **h**: **le huitième**, **la onzième**.

§ 39 Telling Time

Die Uhrzeit

Here's how the complete hours, the half hours, and the quarter hours are given in daily speech:

Il est deux heures.
It is two o'clock.
Il est deux heures et quart.
It is two-fifteen / quarter-past two.
Il est deux heures et demie.
It is two-thirty / half-past two.
Il est trois heures moins le quart.
It is quarter to three / two forty-five.

Here's how to tell time using the 24-hour clock:

Il est treize heures vingt-cinq.
It is 1:25 P.M.
Il est vingt heures trente.
It is 8:30 P.M.
Il est vingt-trois heures quarante-cinq.
It is 11:45 P.M. / quarter to midnight.

The preposition **à** is used to specify a time of day:

Je te téléphone à huit heures, d'accord ?

§ 40 Prefixes

The Prefix *re-*

The prefix **re-** can be used to indicate repetition:
voir / revoir *(to see / see again)*.

Before verbs with a vowel at the beginning, **re-** changes to **r-** or **ré-**:
appeler / rappeler *(to call / call back or again)*
apprendre / réapprendre *(to learn / to relearn or learn again)*.

Before verbs with an **s** at the beginning, **re-** changes to **res-**:
sortir / ressortir *(to go out / go back out)*.

§ 41 Apostrophe

If a preposition, pronoun, article, etc. (**de**, **se**, **le** . . .) is followed by a word that starts with a vowel (**a**, **e**, or **i**) or a mute **h**, the preposition, pronoun, article, etc., is shortened with an apostrophe:
d'Angleterre
s'appeler
l'italien
qu'est-ce que ... ?

A

	... heures de l'après-midi	... o'clock in the afternoon
	... heures du matin	... o'clock in the morning
	... heures du soir	... o'clock in the evening
	..., non ?	..., right?
	a	(he / she) has
	à	in
	à	at
	à	to
	à	up to
	à ... heures du matin	at ... o'clock in the morning
	à bientôt	see you soon
	à cause de	because of
	à côté de	beside
	à droite	to the right
	à gauche	to the left
	à la carte	à la carte
	à la française	French-style
	à la maison	house-style
	à mon âge	at my age
	à partir de	starting with
	à pied	on foot
	A quelle heure ?	At what time?
	à qui ?	to whom?
	absolument	absolutely
	acheter	to buy
l'	acteur (m.)	actor
	actif	active, lively
	active	active
l'	actrice (f.)	actress
	adorer	to adore, worship
l'	adresse (f.)	address
l'	aéroport (m.)	airport
l'	affaire (f.)	thing
les	affaires (f.)	things
les	affaires de toilette (f.)	toiletries
l'	âge (m.)	age
l'	agenda (f.)	appointment calendar
	agir	to act

	Ah !	Ah!
	Ah bon !	Ah!
	Ah oui !	Oh, yes!
	Ah ! Le voilà !	Ah! There he / it is!
	ai	(I) have
	aider	to help
	aimable	friendly
	aimer (+ infinitive)	to like to do something
	aimer (+ noun)	to like / love
l'	airbus (m.)	Airbus
	ajouter	to add
l'	alcool	alcohol
l'	Algérie (f.)	Algeria
l'	Algérien (m.)	Algerian (m.)
l'	Algérienne (f.)	Algerian (f.)
l'	Allemand (m.)	German (m.)
l'	Allemande (f.)	German (f.)
	aller	to go
	aller bien	to be well
	aller chercher	to pick up
	aller en avion	to go by plane
	aller en train	to go by train
	aller en voiture	to go by car
	aller mal	to be ill, to go badly
	aller voir	to go see
	aller voir	to visit
l'	aller-retour (m.)	round trip
	allez	(you) go
	Allez !	Come on!
	Allô ?	Hello (anwering telephone
	allons	(we) go; let's go
	alors	thus
les	Alpes (w. / Pl.)	the Alps
	amener	to bring
l'	Américain (m.)	American (m.)
l'	Américaine (f.)	American (f.)
l'	ami (m.)	friend (m.)
l'	amie (f.)	friend (f.)
l'	amour (m.)	love
s'	amuser	to have fun, amuse oneself
l'	an (m.)	year
l'	ananas (m.)	pineapple

l'	Anglais *(m.)*	Englishman
l'	Anglaise *(f.)*	Englishwoman
l'	Angleterre *(f.)*	England
l'	animal *(m.)*	animal
l'	année *(f.)*	year
l'	anniversaire *(m.)*	birthday
	août *(m.)*	August
l'	apéritif *(m.)*	aperitif
l'	apostrophe *(f.)*	apostrophe
l'	appareil photo *(m.)*	camera
l'	appartement *(m.)*	apartment
s'	appeler	to be named / called
	appeler	to call
	apprendre	to learn
	appris	learned
	après	after
	après-demain	the day after tomorrow
l'	après-midi *(m./f.)*	afternoon
l'	arabe *(m.)*	Arabic (language)
l'	architecte *(m./f.)*	architect
les	Ardennes *(f.)*	the Ardennes
l'	argent *(m.)*	money
l'	armoire *(f.)*	closet
	arrêter	to stop
	arriver	to arrive
l'	arrondissement	precinct
	as	(you) have
l'	Asie *(f.)*	Asia
	assez	enough
	assez	rather, quite
l'	assiette *(f.)*	plate
	attendre	to wait
	attends	wait
	au	to the (à + le)
	au	in (à + le)
	au bord de la mer	at the seashore
	au milieu de	in the middle
	au revoir	good-bye
l'	auditeur *(m.)*	listener *(m.)*
l'	auditrice *(f.)*	listener *(f.)*
	aujourd'hui	today
	aussi	also
	aussi ... que	as . . .as
l'	autoroute *(f.)*	highway
	autre *(m./f.)*	other
l'	Autriche *(f.)*	Austria
l'	Autrichien *(m.)*	Austrian man
l'	Autrichienne *(f.)*	Austrian woman
	avancer	to advance
	avant	before
	avant-hier	the day before yesterday
	avec	with
	avec plaisir	gladly
l'	avenue *(f.)*	avenue
l'	avenue Daumesnil	Daumesnil Avenue
	avez	(you) have
l'	avion *(m.)*	airplane
	avoir	to have
	avoir besoin de	to need
	avoir de la chance	to be lucky
	avoir faim	to be hungry
	avoir froid	to be cold
	avoir le temps	to have the time
	avoir mal	to have a pain
	avoir mal à la tête	to have a headache
	avoir mal au ventre	to have a stomachache
	avoir son train	to catch one's train
	avons	(we) have
l'	avril	April

B

le	bac	baccalaureate degree
le	badminton	badminton
la	baguette	baguette
le	balcon	balcony
la	balle	ball
le	ballon	ball
la	banane	banana
la	banque	bank
le	bar	bar
le	basket	basketball
le	basket-ball	basketball
la	Bastille	Bastille
le	bateau	boat, ship
	beau	beautiful, handsome
	Beauchamp	Beauchamp

	beaucoup	*very*		la	bouteille	*bottle*
	beaucoup	*much*			bronzé	*tanned*
	bel	*beautiful, handsome*			bronzée	*tanned*
	Belaoui	*Belaoui*		la	brosse à dents	*toothbrush*
le	belge	*Belgian (language)*			brun	*dark-haired, brunette*
le	Belge *(m.)*	*Belgian man*			brune	*brunette*
la	Belge *(f.)*	*Belgian woman*			Bruxelles	*Brussels*
la	Belgique	*Belgium*			bu	*drunk*
	belle	*beautiful*		le	bureau	*office*
	ben, oui	*Well, yes*		le	bureau	*desk*
le	beurre	*butter*		le	bus	*bus*
	bien	*well*				
	bien sûr	*of course*				
	bientôt	*soon*		**C**		
la	bière	*beer*			ça	*that*
	bilingue	*bilingual*			ça va	*OK*
le	billet	*ticket*			Ça y est!	*That's it!*
le	billet d'avion	*airplane ticket*		le	cadeau	*gift*
le	billet de train	*train ticket*		le	café	*coffee*
	bio	*organic*		le	café	*café*
la	biologie	*biology*		la	caméra	*camera*
	blanc	*white*		la	campagne	*country*
	blanche	*white*		le	Canada	*Canada*
le	bleu	*blue*		le	Canadien	*Canadian (m.)*
	bleu	*blue*		la	Canadienne	*Canadian (f.)*
	bleue	*blue*		le	canal Saint-Martin	*Saint Martin Canal*
	blond	*blond*		le	caniche	*poodle*
	blonde	*blond*			Carcassonne	*Carcassonne*
	boire	*to drink*			Caroline	*Caroline*
la	boisson	*drink*		la	carte	*menu, map*
	bon	*good*		la	carte (postale)	*(post)card*
	bon appétit	*Enjoy your meal.*		la	carte de crédit	*credit card*
	bon marché	*cheap*			Casablanca	*Casablanca*
	Bon, ...	*Well, . . .*		le	cassis	*black currante*
le	bonbon	*candy*			Catherine	*Catherine*
	bonjour	*hello*		le	CD	*CD*
	bonne	*good*			ce	*this*
	Bordeaux	*Bordeaux*			ce matin	*this morning*
	bouger	*to move*			Ce n'est pas grave.	*It's not serious.*
le	boulanger	*baker (m.)*			ce samedi	*this Saturday*
la	boulangère	*baker (f.)*			ce soir	*this evening*
la	boulangerie	*bakery*			ce sont	*they are*
le	boulevard	*boulevard*		la	cédille	*cedilla*
le	bouquet	*bouquet*			cela	*that*

	célèbre	*famous*
le	célibataire	*bachelor*
la	célibataire	*unmarried woman*
	cent	*hundred*
	cent un	*a hundred and one*
le / la	centième	*hundredth*
	ces	*these*
	c'est	*it is*
	c'est dommage	*That's a shame*
	C'est plus facile à dire qu'à faire.	*Easier said than done.*
	cet	*this*
	cette	*this*
la	chaise	*chair*
la	chambre	*room, bedroom*
la	chance	*luck*
	changer	*to change*
se	changer	*to change clothes*
	changer	*to change*
	changer	*to change, transfer*
	chanter	*to sing*
le	chapeau	*hat*
le	chaperon	*hood*
	chaque	*each*
	chaque jour	*every day*
	Charlotte	*Charlotte*
le	chat	*cat*
	Château-Chinon	*Château-Chinon*
la	chatte	*female cat*
la	chaussure	*shoe*
le	chef	*chef*
le	chef cuisinier	*head chef*
la	cheminée	*chimney*
la	chemise	*shirt*
	cher	*expensive*
	cher	*dear*
	chercher	*to look for*
	chère	*expensive*
	chère	*dear*
le	cheval	*horse*
le	cheveu	*hair (individual hair)*
les	cheveux (m./pl.)	*hair*
	chez	*at*
	chez	*at the house of*

	chic	*stylish*
le	chien	*dog (male)*
la	chienne	*female dog*
la	Chine	*China*
le	Chinois	*Chinese man*
le	chinois	*Chinese (language)*
	chinois	*Chinese*
la	Chinoise	*Chinese woman*
	chinoise	*Chinese*
les	chips	*potato chips*
	Chléo	*Chléo*
	Chloé	*Chloé*
le	chocolat	*chocolate*
la	chocolaterie	*cholocate shop, candy shop*
	choisir	*to choose*
	Christine	*Christine*
le	cinéma	*movie*
	cinq	*five*
	cinq cents	*five hundred*
	cinquante	*fifty*
	cinquante-neuf	*fifty-nine*
le / la	cinquième	*fifth*
la	classe	*class*
la	classe affaires	*business class*
	Claude	*Claude*
la	clé	*key*
la	clef	*key*
le	client	*client, customer (m.)*
la	cliente	*client, customer (f.)*
le	cochon	*pig*
le	coiffeur	*hairdresser, barber*
la	coiffeuse	*hairdresser (f.)*
le	collègue	*colleague (m.)*
la	collègue	*colleague (f.)*
	combien	*how much*
	combien de temps?	*how long?*
	comme	*like*
	comme	*as*
	commencer	*to begin*
	comment	*how*
	comment?	*what?*
	Comment allez-vous ?	*How are you?*

	Comment ça se fait ?	*How is that possible?*
	Comment vas-tu ?	*How are you?*
	complet	*full*
	complet	*complete*
	complète	*complete, full*
	complète	*complete*
	complètement	*completely*
	comprendre	*to understand*
le	compte (en banque)	*account*
	conduire	*to drive, lead*
	confortable	*comfortable*
	connais	*(I) know*
	connais	*you know*
la	connaissance	*acquaintance / knowledge*
	connaissent	*(they) know*
	connaissez	*(you) know*
	connaissons	*(we) know*
	connaît	*(he, she, one) knows*
	connaître	*to know*
se	connaître	*to know one another*
	connu	*known*
le	conseil	*advice*
	conservateur	*conservative, old-fashioned*
	conservatrice	*conservative, old-fashioned*
	content	*happy*
	contente	*happy*
le	contrat	*contract*
	contre	*against*
les	coordonnées (f./pl.)	*personal data*
le	copain	*friend*
la	copine	*friend (f.)*
la	Corse	*Corsica*
la	Côte d'Azur	*Côte d'Azur*
se	coucher	*to go to bed*
la	couleur	*color*
	couramment	*fluently*
le	coureur	*runner*
la	coureuse	*runner (f.)*

	courir	*to run*
le	cours	*course*
	court	*short*
	courte	*short*
	couru	*run*
le	cousin	*cousin (m.)*
la	cousine	*cousin (f.)*
	coûter	*to cost*
la	crème solaire	*suntan lotion*
la	crêpe	*crêpe*
	Créteil	*Créteil*
	croient	*(they) believe*
	croire	*to believe*
	crois	*(I) believe*
	crois	*you believe*
le	croissant	*croissant*
	croit	*(he, she, one) believes*
	croyez	*(you) believe*
	croyons	*(we) believe*
	cru	*believed*
la	cuillère	*spoon*
la	cuisine	*kitchen*

D

	d'abord	*first*
	d'accord	*agreed*
	dans	*in*
	dans ce cas	*in that case*
	danser	*to dance*
le	danseur	*dancer (m.)*
la	danseuse	*dancer (f.)*
	d'autres	*other*
	de	*partitive article*
	de	*from*
	de ... à	*from ... to*
	de l'	*from / partitive article*
	de la	*partitive article*
le	début	*beginning*
	décembre	*December*
	déçu / e	*disappointed*
	déjà	*already*
le	déjeuner	*lunch*

	demain	tomorrow
	demander	to ask
	demander conseil	to ask for advice
	demi / e	half
la	demi-heure	half hour
le	dentifrice	toothpaste
le	dentiste	dentist
la	dentiste	dentist (f.)
le	départ	departure
	depuis	since
	dernier	last
	dernière	last
	derrière	behind
	des	plural form of indefinite article
la	destination	destination
	détester qc	to hate something / dislike something
	deux	two
	deux cents	two hundred
	deux fois	twice
	deux mille quatre	two thousand four
le / la	deuxième	second
la	deuxième fois	second time / for the second time
	devant	in front of
	devenir	to become
	devenu	become
	devez	(you) must
	devoir	to have to, must
	devons	(we) must
la	différence	difference
	difficile	difficult
le	dîner	dinner
	dire	to say
	directement	directly, immediately
le	directeur	director
la	directrice	director (f.)
	dis	(I) say
	dis	(you) say
	discret	discreet, reserved
	discrète	discreet, reserved
	disent	(they) say
	disons	(we) say
	disons	let us say

	disparaître	to disappear
	disparu	disappeared
le	disque	record
la	disquette	diskette
	dit	(he, she, one) says
	dites	(you) say
	dix	ten
	dix-huit	eighteen
	dix-neuf	nineteen
	dix-sept	seventeen
le	docteur	doctor
	dois	(I) must
	dois	(you) must
	doit	(they) must
	doivent	must
	Dominique	Dominique
	donc	thus
	donner	to give
	donner à manger	to feed
	dormir	to sleep
	d'où?	from where?
	douze	twelve
	drôle	funny
	du	from
	du	partitive article
	dû	past participle of devoir, to have to, must
	Dupont	Dupont
	durer	to last
	Duval	Duval

E

l'	eau (f.)	water
l'	eau gazeuse (f.)	carbonated water
l'	eau plate (f.)	noncarbonated water
	échanger	to exchange
l'	école (f.)	school
	écouter	to listen to
	écrire	to write
l'	église (f.)	church
	élégant	elegant
	élégante	elegant
	elle	she

	elle	she, her, accentuating personal pronoun			étranger	foreign
				l'	étranger (m.)	foreigner
	elles	they			étrangère	foreign
	emmener	to take		l'	étrangère (f.)	foreign (f.)
l'	employé / e	employee			être	to be
	en	in			être désolé / e	to be sorry
	en	of			je suis (tu es /	I am / you are /
	en	to			il est) désolé / e	he is sorry
	en	in the year		les	études (f. / pl.)	studies
	en face	facing		l'	étudiant (m.)	student
	en tout cas	in any case		l'	étudiante (f.)	student (f.)
	enchanté / e	pleased (to meet you)			étudier	to study
	encore	still			eu	had
s'	endormir	to fall asleep			Euh	Uh . . .
l'	enfance (f.)	childhood		l'	euro (m.)	Euro
l'	enfant (m.)	child		l'	Europe (f.)	Europe
	ennuyeuse	boring			européen	European
	ennuyeux	boring			européenne	European
	ensemble	together			eux	they, them— accentuating personal pronoun
	ensuite	then				
	entendre	to hear				
	entre	between			évidemment	obviously
	entre	among			exactement	exactly
	entre	during		l'	excuse (f.)	excuse
l'	entreprise (f.)	business, company			excuse-moi	excuse my
l'	entreprise d'infor- matique (f.)	computer business			excusez-moi	excuse me
				l'	expert (m.)	expert (m.)
l'	enveloppe (f.)	envelope		l'	experte (f.)	expert (f.)
l'	épicerie (f.)	grocery store				
l'	équipe (f.)	team		**F**		
	es	(you) are				
l'	Espagne (f.)	Spain			facilement	easily
l'	espagnol (m.)	Spanish (language)		le	facteur	mail carrier
	espérer	to hope			faible	weak
	est	(he, she) is			faire	to make, to do
	est-ce que ?	expression used in asking a question			faire ce qu'on peut	to do what one can
					faire de la gymnastique	to do gymnastics
	et	and				
l'	Etat (m.)	state			faire de la musique	to play music
les	Etats-Unis (m. / Pl.)	United States			faire de la natation	to swim
	été	been			faire des bêtises	to do dumb things
l'	été (m.)	summer			faire du (36)	to take clothing / shoe size 36
	êtes	(you) are				
l'	étranger	foreign country			faire du bruit	to make noise

	faire du cheval	to go horseback riding		finir	to finish
	faire du piano	to play the piano	se	finir	to end
	faire du ski	to ski	la	fleur	flower
	faire du sport	to play sports		Florence	Florence
	faire du tennis	to play tennis		font	(they) make / do
	faire la connais- sance de qn	to meet someone	le	football	soccer
				fort	strong
	faire la cuisine	to cook		fort	here: good
	faire la vaisselle	to do the dishes		forte	strong
	faire le ménage	to do the housework		forte	here: good
	faire les courses	to go shopping	le	Français	Frenchman
	faire mal	to hurt	le	français	French (language)
	faire qc dans la vie	to do something professionally		français	French
				française	French
	faire ses devoirs	to do one's homework	la	Française	Frenchwoman
	faire un gâteau	to bake a cake	la	France	France
	faire un stage	to do training		Francine	Francine
	fais	(I) make / do		François Delaunay	François Delaunay
	fais	(you) make / do		Franz	Franz
	faisons	(we) make / do		Frédéric	Frédéric
	fait	(he, she) makes / does		Frédérique	Frédérique
	fait	done / made	le	frère	brother
	faites	(you) make / do	le	frigidaire	refrigerator
	Faites comme chez vous!	Make yourself at home!	les	frites (w./Pl.)	French fries
			le	fromage	cheese
	falloir	to have to / must		fumer	to smoke
la	famille	family			
la	farine	flour		**G**	
	fatigant	tiring			
	fatigante	tiring		Gaëlle	Gaëlle
	fatigué / e	tired		gagner	to win
	Fatiha	Fatiha	le	garage	garage
le	fauteuil	armchair	le	garçon	boy
la	femme	woman		garder	here: to look after
la	femme	wife	la	gare	railroad station
la	femme docteur	woman doctor		Gaston	Gaston
la	femme ingénieur	woman engineer	le	gâteau	cake
la	femme médecin	woman doctor		genial	nice
	fermer	to close		géniale	nice
la	fête	holiday, party		gentil	nice
la	Fête du Travail	Workers' Day		gentille	nice
	fêter	to celebrate	le	goûter	snack
la	fille	daughter	le	gramme	gram
le	film	film		grand	large

	grand	*great*
	grande	*large*
	grande	*great*
les	grandes vacances	*summer vacation*
	grandir	*to grow*
la	grand-mère	*grandmother*
	gratuit	*free*
	gratuite	*free*
	grave	*serious, grave*
	Grenoble	*Grenoble*
la	grève	*strike*
	gris	*gray*
	grise	*gray*
	gros	*fat*
	grosse	*fat*
la	guitare	*guitar*
la	gymnastique	*gymnastics*

H

	Ha, ha	*Ha ha*
s'	habiller	*to get dressed*
	habiter	*to live*
	Hein ?	*Huh?*
	Hein ?	*right?*
l'	heure *(f.)*	*hour, time*
	heureuse	*happy*
	heureusement	*fortunately*
	heureux	*happy*
	hier	*yesterday*
l'	histoire *(f.)*	*story, history*
l'	homme *(m.)*	*man*
	Honfleur	*Honfleur*
l'	hôpital *(m.)*	*hospital*
l'	hôtel *(m.)*	*hotel*
l'	Hôtel de la Pitié	*l'Hôtel de la Pitié*
	huit	*eight*
le / la huitième		*eighth*

I

	ici	*here*
l'	idée *(f.)*	*idea*
	il	*he*
	Il est ... heures.	*It is . . .o'clock.*

	il fait ... degrés	*It is . . . degrees.*
	il fait beau	*It's nice out.*
	il fait chaud	*The weather is warm / hot.*
	il fait froid	*It's cold out.*
	il fait mauvais	*The weather is lousy.*
	il faut	*(il faut + infinitive) one must*
	il faut (+ noun)	*. . . is needed / required*
	il manque	*. . . is lacking / missing*
	il me faut	*il me faut (+ noun) I need*
	il n'y a pas de ...	*There is / are no . . .*
	il n'y en a plus	*There is / are no more*
	il pleut	*It is raining.*
	il y a	*there is / there are*
	il y a	*here: ago*
	Il y en a	*There are some*
l'	île *(f.)*	*island*
l'	île *(f.)* de Ré	*Isle of Ré*
	ils	*they*
	important	*important*
	importante	*important*
l'	informatique	*computer science*
	informatique	*computer*
l'	ingénieur *(m.)*	*engineer*
l'	ingrédient	*ingredient*
s'	installer	*to settle into*
l'	instrument *(m.)*	*musical instrument*
	intéressant	*interesting*
	intéressante	*interesting*
l'	interview *(f.)*	*interview*
l'	invité *(m.)*	*guest*
l'	invitée *(f.)*	*female guest*
	inviter	*to invite*
l'	Italie *(f.)*	*Italy*
l'	Italien *(m.)*	*Italian man*
l'	Italienne *(f.)*	*Italian woman*

J

	Jane	*Jane*
le	janvier	*January*

	japonais	*Japanese*
	japonaise	*Japanese*
le	jardin	*garden*
le	jardinier	*gardener*
la	jardinière	*gardener*
	jaune	*yellow*
le	jaune	*yellow (color)*
le	jaune d'oeuf	*egg yolk*
le	jazz	*jazz*
	je	*I*
	Je n'en peux plus.	*I've had it.*
	Je peux vous aider?	*May I help you?*
	je voudrais (+ infinitive)	*I would like*
	je voudrais (+ noun)	*I would like*
	Jean	*Jean*
	Jean-Marie	*Jean-Marie*
	Jeanne	*Jeanne*
	Jeanne-Marie	*Jeanne-Marie*
	Jean-Pierre	*Jean-Pierre*
	jeune	*young*
	Jimi Hendrix	*Jimi Hendrix*
	Joel	*Joel*
	Joelle	*Joelle*
	Johnny	*Johnny*
	joli / e	*pretty*
	jouer	*to play*
	jouer au tennis	*to play tennis*
	jouer du piano	*to play the piano*
	jouer d'un instrument	*to play an instrument*
le	joueur	*player*
le	joueur de tennis	*tennis player*
la	joueuse	*player (f.)*
la	joueuse de tennis	*tennis player (f.)*
le	jour	*day*
le	journal	*newspaper*
le	journalisme	*journalism*
le	journaliste	*journalist*
la	journaliste	*journalist*
	joyeuse	*joyful*
	joyeux	*happy*
le	juillet	*July*

	Julia	*Julia*
	Julie	*Julie*
	Julien	*Julien*
le	jus	*juice*
le	jus d'orange	*orange juice*
	jusque	*until*
	jusqu'ici	*so far*
	juste là	*right there*

K

le	kilo	*kilo*

L

	la	*the*
	là	*there*
	-là	*(celui-là) that one*
	la nuit	*at night*
	La Rochelle	*La Rochelle*
	là-bas	*over there*
	laid	*ugly*
	laide	*ugly*
	laisser	*to leave*
le	lait	*milk*
le	latin	*Latin (language)*
	Laura	*Laura*
	Laure	*Laure*
se	laver	*to wash (oneself)*
	le	*the*
	le matin	*in the morning, every morning*
	Le Monde	*Le Monde*
	Le Pré-Saint-Gervais	*Le Pré-Saint-Gervais*
	le samedi	*every Saturday*
	le week-end	*every weekend*
	le / la / les	*definite articles*
la	leçon	*lessons*
	lent	*slow*
	lente	*slow*
	les	*plural definite article*
la	lettre	*letter*
	leur	*their*
	leur	*to / for them / their*

	leurs	*their*
	lever	*to live*
se	lever	*to get up*
	libre	*free*
la	ligne	*airline*
la	ligne	*line*
la	limonade	*lemonade*
	lire	*to read*
le	lit	*bed*
le	livre	*book*
	loin	*far, distant*
	Londres	*London*
	long	*long*
	longtemps	*long time*
	longue	*long*
	Louis XIV	*Louis XIV*
le	Louvre	*the Louvre (Museum in Paris)*
	lu	*read*
	lui	*he*
	lui	*to / for him / her*
le	lundi	*Monday*
	lundi matin	*Monday morning*
la	lune	*moon*
les	lunettes *(f. / Pl.)*	*glasses*
les	lunettes de soleil *(f. / Pl.)*	*sunglasses*
	Lyon	*Lyon*

M

	M.	*abbreviation of Monsieur (Mr.)*
	ma	*my*
	Madame	*Madame (direct address)*
	Mademoiselle	*Miss (direct address)*
	Madrid	*Madrid*
le	magasin	*store*
le	magasin de chaussures	*shoe store*
	magnifique	*wonderful*
	mai	*May*
le	maillot de bain	*bathing suit*
la	main	*hand*

	maintenant	*now*
	mais	*but*
	Mais si !	*Oh, yes!*
la	maison	*house*
la	maison blanche	*White House*
	mal	*bad*
	malade	*sick*
la	mamie	*grandma (term of endearment)*
	manger	*to eat*
la	manifestation	*demonstration*
	manquer	*to be lacking, missing*
le	manteau	*overcoat*
	Marc	*Marc*
le	marchand	*dealer*
la	marchande	*dealer (f.)*
	marcher	*to walk*
le	mardi	*Tuesday*
	mardi après-midi	*Tuesday afternoon*
	mardi matin	*Tuesday morning*
le	mari	*husband*
le	mariage	*marriage*
	Marie	*Marie*
	marié / e	*married*
se	marier	*to get married*
	Marie-Sophie	*Marie-Sophie*
le	Maroc	*Morocco*
le	Marocain	*Moroccan man*
	marocain	*Moroccan*
	marocaine	*Moroccan*
la	Marocaine	*Moroccan woman*
	marquer	*to mark*
	marron	*brown*
	Marseille	*Marseille*
	Martin	*Martin*
le	match	*game, match*
les	mathématiques	*mathematics*
	Mathieu	*Mathieu*
	Mathilde	*Mathilde*
le	matin	*morning*
	mauvais	*bad*
	mauvaise	*bad*
	me	*me*
le	médecin	*doctor*
le	meilleur	*best*

	meilleur	*better*
la	meilleure	*best*
	meilleure	*better*
	mélanger	*to mix*
	même	*even*
la	mer	*sea*
la	Mercedes	*Mercedes*
	merci	*thanks*
le	mercredi	*Wednesday*
la	mère	*mother*
la	merguez	*merguez (small spicy paprika sausage made from lamb)*
	mes	*my*
le	métro	*subway*
	mettre	*to put, place, lay, hang*
	mettre	*here: to put on*
le	Mexicain	*Mexican man*
le	mexicain	*Mexican (language)*
la	Mexicaine	*Mexican woman*
le	Mexique	*Mexico*
	Michel	*Michel*
	Michèle	*Michèle*
le	midi	*noon, south*
	mieux	*better*
	mille neuf cent quatre-vingt quatorze	*1994*
	mille neuf cent soixante-quatorze	*1974*
	mille neuf cents quatre-vingt trois	*1983*
	mille neuf cents soixante-treize	*1973*
	Minou	*pussy-cat*
le	minuit *(m.)*	*midnight*
la	minute	*minute*
	mis	*here: put on*
	Mlle	*abbreviation of mademoiselle*
	Mme	*abbreviation of Madame*

	moi	*I (without verb), me (with preposition)*
	moindre	*lesser*
	moins	*less, minus*
	moins	*here: before*
	moins ... que	*less . . .than*
	moins le quart	*quarter to (in telling time)*
le	mois	*month*
le	moment	*moment*
	mon	*my*
le	monde	*world*
	Monsieur	*Mister (direct address)*
la	montagne	*mountains*
	Montmartre	*Montmartre*
la	montre	*watch*
	Montréal	*Montreal*
la	moto	*motorcycle*
	Moulin	*Moulin*
	Mounier	*Mounier*
	Mounir	*Arabian man's first name*
la	mousse	*foam*
la	mousse au chocolat	*chocolate mousse*
le	musée	*museum*
le	musée des Beaux-Arts	*fine arts museum*
le	musicien	*musician*
la	musicienne	*musician (f.)*
la	musique	*music*

N

	Nadège	*Nadège*
	nager	*to swim*
	naître	*to be born*
	naturel	*natural*
	naturelle	*natural*
	naturellement	*naturally*
	né	*born*
	ne ... aucun	*no, none*
	ne ... aucune	*no, none*
	ne ... jamais	*never*
	ne ... personne	*no one, nobody*
	ne ... plus	*no longer*

	ne ... rien	nothing
	ne ... pas	not
	ne ... plus	no longer
	ne rien faire	to do nothing
	Ne t'en fais pas !	Don't worry!
	né/e (m./f.)	born
	née	born
	N'est-ce pas ?	right? isn't it? etc.
	neuf	nine
le/la	neuvième	ninth
	New York	New York
le	nez	nose
	Nice	Nice
	Nicolas	Nicholas
	Nirvana	Nirvana
le	Noël (m.)	Christmas
	noir	black
	noire	black
le	nom	name
	non	no
	non plus	no
	non, merci	no, thanks
la	Normandie	Normandy
	notre	our
	Notre-Dame	Notre-Dame
	nous	we
	nous	us
	nouveau	new
	nouvel	new (masculine, before vowel)
	nouvelle	new
le	nuage	cloud
la	nuit	night
le	numéro	number
le	numéro de compte	account number

O

	octobre (m.)	October
l'	oeuf (m.)	egg
l'	oeil (m.)	eye
	offert	given, offered
l'	offre (f.)	offering
	offrir	to offer

	offrir	to give
	Oh ...	Oh . . .
	Oh là là !	Ay, ay, ay!
	Oh non !	Oh, no!
	on	one, we
	on va	we go
	On y va !	Let's go. Off we go!
l'	oncle (m.)	uncle
	ont	(they) have
	onze	eleven
le/la	onzième	eleventh
	orange	orange (colored)
l'	orange (f.)	orange
l'	ordinateur (m.)	computer
	organiser	to organize
	où	where
	oublier	to forget
	oui	yes
	ouvrir	to open

P

	Pablo	Pablo
les	pages blanches	telephone book in France
les	pages jaunes	yellow pages
le	pain	bread
la	paire	pair
le	pantalon	pants
la	panthère	panther
la	panthère rose	Pink Panther
	papa	dad
	Pâques (f./Pl.)	Easter
le	paquet	packet, package
	par	here: per
le	parapluie	umbrella
le	parc	park
le	parc des Buttes-Chaumont	Buttes-Chaumont-Park
	parce que	because
les	parents	parents
les	parents	relatives
	parfait	perfect
	parfaite	perfect

	parfois	sometimes			petite	small
	Paris	Paris		la	petite-fille	granddaughter
le	Parisien	Parisian		le	petit-four	delicious pastry
	parisien	Parisian		la	Peugeot	Peugeot
la	Parisienne	Parisian woman			peut	(he, she, one) can
	parisienne	Parisian			peut-être	perhaps
	parler	to speak		la	photo	photo
	partir	to leave, depart		le	photographe	photograph
	partir en famille	to go away with the family		la	photographe	photographer
				la	phrase	sentence
	partir en vacances	to leave for vacation		la	physique	physics
	partout	everywhere		le	piano	piano
	pas	here: not		la	pièce	piece
	pas de	no, none of		la	pièce de monnaie	coin
	pas encore	not yet		le	pied	foot
	Pas moi !	Not I!			Pierre	Pierre
	pas vraiment	not really		le	pilote	pilot
	Pascal	Pascal		la	pilote	pilot (f.)
	Pascale	Pascale		le	ping-pong	ping-pong
	passer	to spend			pire	worse
	passer	to pass, go by		la	piscine	swimming pool
	passer	to pass		la	place	seat
le	pastis	pastis		la	place économique	economy class seat
la	pâte	dough		la	plage	beach
la	pause déjeuner	lunch break		le	plan de ville	map of the city
	pauvre	poor		le	plat	dish
	pauvre	poor, unfortunate		le	plat du jour	daily special
	payer	to pay		le	play-boy	playboy
le	pays	country			plus ... que	more . . . than
le	péage	tollbooth on highway		la	poêle	pan
	pendant	during, while		la	pomme	apple
	penser	to think		le	pont de Bercy	Bercy Bridge
	perdre	to lose		la	porte	door
le	père	father			porter	to carry
	Perpignan	Perpignan		le	Portugais	Portuguese man
la	personne	person		la	Portugaise	Portuguese woman
	Personne ne ...	nobody . . .		le	Portugal	Portugal
la	pétanque	game of boules			poser	here: to ask
	petit	small, little			poser des questions sur ...	to ask questions about someone, something
le	petit chaperon rouge	Little Red Riding Hood				
le	petit pain au chocolat	chocolate biscuit		la	poste	mail
					poster	to send, mail
le	petit-déjeuner	breakfast		le	poulet au basilic	chicken with basil

	pour	(pour + noun) for
	pour	(pour + infinitive) in order to
	pour	here: because of
	pour le moment	for now
	pourcent	percent
	pourquoi	why
	Pourquoi pas ?	why not?
	pouvoir	to be able
	pratique	practical
	précis	precise
	précise	precise
	préférer	to prefer
le	premier	first
la	première	first
la	première fois	the first time
	prend	(he, she, one) takes
	prendre	to take
	prendre des vacances	to take a vacation
	prendre le petit-déjeuner	to have breakfast
	prendre rendez-vous	to set a date
	prends	(I) take
	prends	(you) take
	prenez	take
	prennent	(they) take
	prenons	we take
	préparer	to prepare
	près de	near
	présenter	to present
	presque	almost
	prêt	ready
	prête	ready
le	printemps	spring
	pris	taken
le	prix	price
le	problème	problem
	prochain	next
	prochaine	next
le	produit	product
le	produit bio	organic product
le	professeur	professor, teacher

la	professeur	professor, teacher (f.)
se	promener	to take a walk
	proposer	to propose
	pu	past participle of pouvoir, to be able
	public	public
	publique	public
	puis	then
le	pull	sweater
les	Pyrénées (m./pl.)	Pyrenees

Q

	quand	if
	quand	when
	quand même	still, just the same
	quarante	forty
	quarante-deux	forty-two
	quarante-huit	forty-eight
le/la	quarante-huitième	the forty-eighth
	quarante-trois	forty-three
le	quart	quarter
le	quart d'heure	quarter hour
le	quartier	neighborhood
	quatorze	fourteen
	quatre	four
	quatre cents sept	four hundred and seven
le	quatre heures	snack
	quatre-vingt-deux	eighty-two
	quatre-vingt-dix-neuf	ninety-nine
	quatre-vingt-onze	ninety-one
	quatre-vingt-quatorze	ninety-four
	quatre-vingt-quatre	eighty-four
	quatre-vingts	eighty
	quatre-vingt-dix	ninety
	quatre-vingt-un	ninety-one
le/la	quatrième	fourth
le	quai de Bercy	quai de Bercy
	que	that
	Que ...	May . . .
	que	that
	quelqu'un	someone

	quel / le	which
	Quelle heure est-il?	What time is it?
	quelque chose	something
	quelques	some
	qu'est-ce que	what
	qui	who
	qui	whom?
la	quiche	quiche
	quinze	fifteen
	quitter	to leave
	quoi	what
	Quoi?	what?

R

le	radiateur	radiator
	ranger	here: to neaten up
	ranger la chambre	rap
le	rap	fast
	rapide	quickly
	rapidement	quickly
	rare	rare
	rarement	rarely
	Raymond	Raymond
la	réalité	reality
la	recette	recipe
le	rédacteur	editor
la	rédactrice	editor (f.)
la	réduction	reduction
	réfléchir	to reflect
	regarde	look
	regarder	to look at, watch
	regarder	to look into
le	régime	diet
la	région	region
	rencontrer	to meet
le	rendez-vous	meeting
	rendre	to return, give back
	rendre visite à qn	to visit someone
	rendu	returned
	René	René
	Renée	Renée
	rentrer	to go back
	rentrer à la maison	to return home

la	réponse	answer
se	reposer	to rest
le	restaurant	restaurant
	rester	to stay, remain
le	retard	delay
	retirer de l'argent	to take out money
le	retour	return
	réussir	to succeed
	revenir	to come back
	revenu	returned
	rêveur	dreamy
	rêveuse	dreamy
	revoir	to see again
le	rideau	curtain
	Rien ne ...	nothing . . .
la	robe	dress
	Rome	Rome
la	rose	rose
	Rouen	Rouen
le	rouge	red (color)
	rouge	red
la	route nationale	national highway
la	rue	street
la	rue Rambouillet	Rambouillet Street
le	Russe	Russian man
la	Russe	Russian woman
le	russe	Russian (language)
la	Russie	Russia

S

	sa	his, her
le	sac	bag
le	Sacré-Cœur	Sacré-Cœur
	sais	(you) know
	sais	(I) know
	sait	(he / she / one) knows
la	salle de sport	fitness center
le	salon	living room
	salut	hi
le	samedi	Saturday
le	sandwich	sandwich
	sans	without / -free

	savent	(they) know		six cent vingt-	six hundred and
	savez	to know / know how		quatre	twenty-four
	savoir	to know	le / la	sixième	sixth
	savons	(we) know	le	ski	ski
	se	himself, herself, oneself, themselves	la	sœur	sister
le	second	second	le	soir	evening
la	seconde	second		soixante	sixty
la	Seconde Guerre Mondiale	Second World War		soixante-dix	seventy
				soixante-dix-huit	seventy-eight
la	Seine	Seine (river that flows through Paris)		soixante-douze	seventy-two
				soixante et onze	seventy-one
	seize	sixteen		soixante et un	sixty-one
le	sel	salt	le	soleil	sun
la	semaine	week	la	solution	solution
la	semaine dernière	last week	la	somme	sum
	sentir	to feel / smell		sommes	(we) are
	sentir bon	to feel good		son	his
	sept	seven		sont	(they) are
le / la	septième	seventh		Sophie	Sophie
le	septième ciel	seventh heaven		sorti / e	gone, left
	sérieuse	serious		sortir	to go out, leave
	sérieusement	seriously	la	soupe	soup
	sérieux	serious	la	souris	mouse
	sers	(you) serve		sous	under
	sers	(I) serve		souvent	often
	servent	(they) serve	la	spécialité	specialty
le	serveur	waiter	le	sport	sport
la	serveuse	waitress		sportif	athletic
	servir	to attend to	le	sportif	athlete
	servir	to serve	la	sportive	athlete (f.)
	servons	(we) serve		sportive	training
	ses	his, her	le	stage	training course
	seul	alone		Stéphane	Stéphane
	seule	alone	le	studio	studio
	seulement	only	le	stylo	pen
le	shampoing	shampoo		su	known
	si	yes, on the contrary	le	sucre	sugar
	si	oh, yes	le	Sud	south
	s'il vous plaît	please	le	Suédois	Swede
	Simian	Simian	la	Suédoise	Swede (f.)
	Simon	Simon		suis	(I) am
	Simone	Simone	le	Suisse	Swiss man
	six	six	la	Suisse	Swiss woman
			la	Suisse	Switzerland

	super	very (coll.)
	super	super (coll.)
	Superman	Superman
le	supermarché	supermarket
	sur	on
	sûr	sure
	sûre	sure
la	surprise	surprise
	surtout	especially
	Susan	Susan
le	sushi	sushi
	sympa	nice, friendly, cozy (coll.)

T

	ta	Yours truly,
la	table	table
la	taille	size (shoes, clothing)
	Tanya	Tanya
la	tante	aunt
	tard	late
la	tarte aux pommes	apple pie
la	tasse	cup
	te	you, to / for you
	te	you
la	techno	techno music
le	tee-shirt	T-Shirt
la	télé(vision)	television
le	téléphone	telephone
le	(téléphone) portable	cell phone
	téléphoner	to telephone
le	temps	time
le	tennis	tennis
	Teresa	Teresa
	tes	Yours truly
la	tête	head
le	thé	tea
	Thomas	Thomas
le	timbre	stamp
	toi	you (without verb), to / for you, you (with preposition)

les	toilettes (f. / Pl.)	toilet
le	toit	roof
la	tomate	tomato
	ton	Yours truly
	tôt	early
	toujours	always
le	Tour de France	Tour de France
la	Tour Eiffel	Eiffel Tower
le	tourisme	tourism
le	touriste	tourist
la	touriste	tourist (f.)
	tourner	here: turn
	tous	all
	tous les jours	every day
	tous les soirs	every evening
	tout	all
	tout	entirely
	tout droit	straight ahead
	tout le temps	all the time
un	tout petit peu	a tiny bit
	tout près d'ici	right close by
	toute	totally
	toutes	all
le	train	train
	tranquillement	calmly
le	travail	work
	travailler	to work
les	travaux	construction
	treize	thirteen
	trente	thirty
	trente-six	thirty-six
	très	very
	triste	sad
	trois	three
	trois fois	three times
le / la	troisième	third
	trop	too / too much
	trouver	to find
	trouver drôle	to find something funny
	tu	you (personal pronoun)

U

	un	a, an
	un	one
	un jour	one day
	un matin	one morning
	un moment	one moment
	un peu de	a little
	une	one
l'	université	university

V

	va	(he / she / one) goes
les	vacances (f. / Pl.)	vacation
	vaincre	to conquer
	vaincu	conquered
je	vais	(I) go / am going
la	valise	suitcase
	valoir	to be worth
	vas	(you) go
le	vase	vase
	vaut	(it) is worth
le	vélo	bicycle
le	vendeur	salesman
la	vendeuse	saleswoman
	vendre	to sell
le	vendredi	Friday
	vendu	sold
	venez	(you) come
	venir	to come
	venir voir qn	to visit someone
	Venise	Venice
	venons	(we) come
	venu	came
le	verre	glass
	vers	toward / around
	vers	in the direction of
	vers	approximately
	vert	green
	verte	green
la	veste	jacket
le	vêtement	clothing
	veulent	(they) wish, want

	veut	(he, she) wants
	veux	(I) want
	veux	(you) want
	vide	empty
la	vie	life
	vieil	old
	vieille	old
	Vienne	Vienna (city in Austria)
	viennent	(they) come
	viens	(you) come
	viens	(I) come
	vient	(he, she, one) comes
	vieux	old
la	ville	city
le	vin	wine
	vingt	twenty
	vingt-deux	twenty-two
	vingt et un	twenty-one
	vingt et une	twenty-one
le / la	vingt et unième	twenty-first
	vingt-quatre	twenty-four
	vingt-six	twenty-six
	vingt-trois	twenty-three
le	violon	violin
la	visite guidée	tour
	vite	fast
	vivre	to live
	voici	her is / her are
	voient	(they) see
	voilà	there is / there are
	voir	to see
	vois	(I) see
	vois	(you) see
le	voisin	neighbor
la	voisine	neighbor (f.)
	voit	(he / she / one) sees
la	voiture	car
la	voiture de sport	sports car
le	vol	flight
	voler	to fly
le	voleur	thief
la	voleuse	thief (f.)
	vont	(they) go
	votre	your / Yours truly

	voulez	*want*
	vouloir	*to want*
	voulons	*(we) want*
	voulu	*wanted*
	vous	*you*
	vous	*you, accentuating personal pronoun*
	vous	*you*
	Vous voulez ...?	*Do you want . . .?*
le	voyage	*trip*
	voyager	*to travel*
	voyez	*(you) see*
	voyons	*(we) see*
	vrai / e	*true*
	vraiment	*really*
	vraiment	*truly*
	vu	*seen*

W

le	week-end	*weekend*

Y

	y	*there*
	y	*to there*
	Yann	*Yann*

Z

	zéro	*zero*
	Zinedine Zidane	*Zinedine Zidane*
	Zurich	*Zurich (city in Switzerland)*

Photo credits:

p. 9 *Collage*—Frank Zuber, Stuttgart /EKS, Inc. Stuttgart / Philipp Ziegler, Stuttgart
p. 11 *Hairdresser*—EKS Inc., Stuttgart
p. 11 *Gardener*—Ingram Publishing, Tattenhall, Chester
p. 11 *Musician*—MEV Publishing, Inc., Augsburg
p. 11 *Architect*—MEV Publishing, Inc., Augsburg
p. 11 *Tennis player*—MEV Publishing, Inc., Augsburg
p. 11 *Photographer*—MEV Publishing, Inc., Augsburg
p. 13 *American flag*—Comstock, Luxemburg
p. 13 *Swiss flag*—Comstock, Luxemburg
p. 13 *Spanish flag*—Comstock, Luxemburg
p. 13 *Italian flag*—Comstock, Luxemburg
p. 13 *Moroccan flag*—Comstock, Luxemburg
p. 14 *Chinese character*—MEV Publishing, Inc., Augsburg
p. 14 *Pyramid*—Mexican Tourist Bureau, Frankfurt
p. 14 *Wilderness*—MEV Publishing, Inc., Augsburg
p. 14 *Russian church*—MEV Publishing, Inc., Augsburg
p. 20 *Television*—Eduard Bader, Esslingen
p. 20 *Violinist*—MEV Publishing, Inc., Augsburg
p. 20 *Badminton player*—Frank Zuber, Stuttgart
p. 20 *Tour scene*—Eduard Bader, Esslingen
p. 20 *Listening to music*—Frank Zuber, Stuttgart
p. 20, 23 *Schoolgirl*—Fotosearch RF (Photodisc), Waukesha
p. 23 *Dancer*—Fotosearch RF (Photodisc), Waukesha
p. 23 *Swimmer*—Corel Corporation, Unterschleissheim
p. 23 *Children*—Eduard Bader, Esslingen
p. 23 *Snow*—MEV Publishing, Inc., Augsburg
p. 23 *Swimming pool*—MEV Publishing, Inc., Augsburg
p. 27 *Coffee*—Philipp Ziegler, Stuttgart
p. 27 *Toothpaste*—Philipp Ziegler, Stuttgart
p. 27 *Lemonade*—Philipp Ziegler, Stuttgart

p. 27 *Mineral water*—Philipp Ziegler, Stuttgart
p. 27 *Oranges*—Philipp Ziegler, Stuttgart
p. 27 *Apples*—Philipp Ziegler, Stuttgart
p. 27 *Tea*—EKS, Inc., Stuttgart
p. 27 *Sugar*—Philipp Ziegler, Stuttgart
p. 28, 35 *Post office*—EKS Inc., Stuttgart
p. 28 *Bank*—EKS Inc., Stuttgart
p. 28, 35 *Supermarket*—EKS Inc., Stuttgart
p. 28 *Grocery store*—EKS Inc., Stuttgart
p. 28 *Stamps*—Emilie Villemagne, Paris
p. 28, 35 *Letters*—Philipp Ziegler, Stuttgart
p. 28 *Toothbrush*—Philipp Ziegler, Stuttgart
p. 28 *Toothpaste*—Philipp Ziegler, Stuttgart
p. 28, 35 *Water*—Philipp Ziegler, Stuttgart
p. 30 *Apples*—Philipp Ziegler, Stuttgart
p. 30 *Butter on a scale*—Philipp Ziegler, Stuttgart
p. 30, 33, 36 *Flour*—Philipp Ziegler, Stuttgart
p. 31 *Collage*—MEV Publishing, Inc., Stuttgart / Fotosearch RF, Wausheka
p. 33, 54 *Butter on scale*—Philipp Ziegler, Stuttgart
p. 33 *Sugar*—Philipp Ziegler, Stuttgart
p. 33, 54 *Salt*—Philipp Ziegler, Stuttgart
p. 33, 54 *Eggs*—Philipp Ziegler, Stuttgart
p. 34 *Cup of coffee*—Philipp Ziegler, Stuttgart
p. 34 *Package of coffee*—Philipp Ziegler, Stuttgart
p. 34 *Ground coffee*—Philipp Ziegler, Stuttgart
p. 34 *Two cups of coffee*—Philipp Ziegler, Stuttgart
p. 34 *Spoonful of coffee*—Philipp Ziegler, Stuttgart
p. 34 *Wine bottle*—EKS Inc., Stuttgart
p. 34, 36 *Glass of wine*—Philipp Ziegler, Stuttgart
p. 34 *Glass of beer*—EKS Inc., Stuttgart
p. 34, 36 *Baguette*—Philipp Ziegler, Stuttgart
p. 34, 36 *Several baguettes*—Creativ Collection, Freiburg
p. 34, 36 *Piece of baguette*—Philipp Ziegler, Stuttgart

Recording, Editing, and Mastering:
Ton in Ton Medienhaus, Stuttgart

Editing:
ARTist Tonstudios, Pfullingen

Voices:
Patrick Baudrand
Sonia Blin
Gilles Floret
Veronique Jäck
Nathalie Karanfilovic
Maxime Kern
Rebecca Simpson
Christelle Souvras
Katharina Stilo
Marie-Christine Thiébaut
Régis Titeca
Denise Usal

CD Track List

1

Track 1 – Exercise 2
Track 2 – Exercise 4
Track 3 – Exercise 5
Track 4 – Exercise 7
Track 5 – Exercise 13

2

Track 6 – Exercise 1
Track 7 – Exercise 3
Track 8 – Exercise 4
Track 9 – Exercise 6
Track 10 – Exercise 8
Track 11 – Exercise 9
Track 12 – Exercise 12

3

Track 13 – Exercise 1
Track 14 – Exercise 2
Track 15 – Exercise 6
Track 16 – Exercise 8
Track 17 – Exercise 11

4

Track 18 – Exercise 1
Track 19 – Exercise 4
Track 20 – Exercise 6
Track 21 – Exercise 8
Track 22 – Exercise 12

5

Track 23 – Exercise 1
Track 24 – Exercise 2
Track 25 – Exercise 7

Test 5

Track 26 – Exercise 3

6

Track 27 – Exercise 2
Track 28 – Exercise 6
Track 29 – Exercise 10

7

Track 30 – Exercise 1
Track 31 – Exercise 14

8

Track 32 – Exercise 1
Track 33 – Exercise 2
Track 34 – Exercise 4
Track 35 – Exercise 8

9

Track 36 – Exercise 2
Track 37 – Exercise 3
Track 38 – Exercise 5
Track 39 – Exercise 6

10

Track 40 – Exercise 1
Track 41 – Exercise 2
Track 42 – Exercise 7
Track 43 – Exercise 13

11

Track 44 – Exercise 1
Track 45 – Exercise 7
Track 46 – Exercise 8

12

Track 47 – Exercise 1
Track 48 – Exercise 2
Track 49 – Exercise 7

Notes

Notes

Notes

3 Foreign Language Series From Barron's!

The **VERB SERIES** offers more than 300 of the most frequently used verbs.
The **GRAMMAR SERIES** provides complete coverage of the elements of grammar.
The **VOCABULARY SERIES** offers more than 3500 words and phrases with their foreign language translations. Each book: paperback.

FRENCH GRAMMAR
ISBN: 0-7641-1351-8
$6.99, Can. $9.99

GERMAN GRAMMAR
ISBN: 0-8120-4296-4
$7.99, Can. $11.50

ITALIAN GRAMMAR
ISBN: 0-7641-2060-3
$6.99, Can. $9.99

JAPANESE GRAMMAR
ISBN: 0-7641-2061-1
$6.95, Can. $9.95

RUSSIAN GRAMMAR
ISBN: 0-8120-4902-0
$7.99, Can. $9.99

SPANISH GRAMMAR
ISBN: 0-7641-1615-0
$6.99, Can. $9.99

FRENCH VERBS
ISBN: 0-7641-1356-9
$6.99, Can. $9.99

GERMAN VERBS
ISBN: 0-8120-4310-3
$8.99, Can. $12.99

ITALIAN VERBS
ISBN: 0-7641-2063-8
$6.99, Can. $8.75

SPANISH VERBS
ISBN: 0-7641-1357-7
$5.95, Can. $8.50

FRENCH VOCABULARY
ISBN: 0-7641-1999-0
$6.99, Can. $9.99

GERMAN VOCABULARY
ISBN: 0-8120-4497-5
$8.99, Can. $11.99

ITALIAN VOCABULARY
ISBN: 0-7641-2190-1
$6.95, Can. $9.95

JAPANESE VOCABULARY
ISBN: 0-8120-4743-5
$8.99, Can. $11.99

RUSSIAN VOCABULARY
ISBN: 0-8120-1554-1
$6.95, Can. $8.95

SPANISH VOCABULARY
ISBN: 0-7641-1985-3
$6.95, Can. $9.95

Barron's Educational Series, Inc.
250 Wireless Blvd., Hauppauge, NY 11788 •
Call toll-free: 1-800-645-3476
In Canada: Georgetown Book Warehouse
34 Armstrong Ave., Georgetown, Ontario L7G 4R9 •
Call toll-free: 1-800-247-7160
www.barronseduc.com
Can. $ = Canadian dollars

LANGUAGE PACKAGES FOR BUSY PEOPLE

LANGUAGES ON THE GO–Level 1

Developing language skills is easy and fun with the *On The Go* program! Two—three CDs in each package feature a friendly, English-speaking narrator who teaches language fundamentals step-by-step. All that's needed is a CD player. The ideal course for people *on the go!*

Each package comes in a handy plastic case:

French ISBN: 7755-9*
$16.95, Can. $24.50

Italian ISBN: 7756-7*
$18.99, Can. $24.50

Spanish ISBN: 7757-5*
$16.95, Can. $24.50

Barron's Educational Series, Inc.
250 Wireless Blvd., Hauppauge, NY 11788
In Canada: Georgetown Book Warehouse
34 Armstrong Ave., Georgetown, Ont. L7G 4R9
Visit our web site at: www.barronseduc.com